# Discovery of Hope

**Biblical Pathways to Addiction Recovery**

# Workbook

**Garland Mark Burgess**

4

ISBN: 0981747426
ISBN-13: 9780981747422

# CONTENTS

# PATHWAY 1
# TRUTH AND HONESTY

## MILSTONE 1
## FIRST THINGS FIRST

**Think about it!**

This area is for writing your thoughts and feelings about the information in this lesson. Please be honest with yourself. This exercise will help you understand and retain what you have read.

Thoughts and Feelings:

_____
_____
_____
_____
_____
_____
_____

Lesson Verse: Psalm 127:1

"Except the LORD build the house, they labour in vain that build it; except the LORD keep the city, the watchman waketh *but* in vain."

## Review

This is where the rubber meets the road. You must ask yourself how you will respond to the lesson.

Choose what you believe is the appropriate answer for you, and/or give an explanation of your answer in the space provided. Circle the answer where appropriate.

8

Ask yourself why you are taking this course. What do you expect from yourself while you take this course?

_____

Why can you not continue going in the same direction with your addiction?

_____

What do you expect from Transformed Life and this course?

_____

Think about what kind of life you want for your future and write it in the space provided.

_____

Have you ever felt that you could not be clean or sober except during rehab?

_____

**TRUE** or **FALSE**

Truth Meter

Answer the following questions to the best of your ability. Some of these questions will be on the test at the end of the Pathway.

1. What does the Scripture verse for Lesson 1 mean?

_____

2. The recovery process is a lifetime commitment to what?

_____

3. What is the definition of "Addiction?"

_____

4. As Christians, how do we define "Recovery?"

_____

5. What is the difference in "Reformation" and "Transformation?"

_____

6. Why do addicts become "institutionalized?"

_____

7. What has the answers for all things that touch our lives?

_____

8. How must we see addictions?

_____

9. What is the Biblical view of addiction recovery?

_____

10. To whom is the power of God available?

_____

11. It is only through what that a person can gain lasting recovery from the bondage of addiction?

_____

12. Yes or No: Does making good decisions make a person good? What are the three things that you should not rely upon? How did God show His love for us? Who paid the penalty for sin that God demanded? What makes your future without life-controlling behaviors possible?

_____

10

**Think about it!**

This area is for writing your thoughts and feelings about the information in this lesson. Please be honest with yourself. This exercise will help you understand and retain what you have read.

Thoughts and Feelings:

_____

_____

_____

_____

_____

_____

_____

_____

_____

_____

_____

**Lesson verse: Psalm 139:14**

"I will fear thee; for I am fearfully and wonderfully made: marvelous are thy works; and that my soul knoweth right well."

## Review

This is where the rubber meets the road. You must ask yourself how you will respond to the lesson.

Choose what you believe is the appropriate answer for you, and/or give an explanation of your answer in the space provided. Circle the answer where appropriate.

What physical condition do you feel you are in currently? Choose from the following scale:

Very poor
Poor
Moderately Poor
Good
Moderately Good
Very Good
Excellent

_____

_____

What do you believe is the main factor that affects your health in a negative way at this time?

Inactivity / Sedentary lifestyle
Substance abuse
Poor eating habits
Lack of medical attention
Lack of exercise
All of the above
None of the above
Other, Explain:

_____

_____

How important do you feel your physical well-being is to your recovery process?

None
Low
Moderate

Important
Very important
Crucial
Not sure

_____

_____

Do you believe God created your physical body the way He did for a specific reason?
Yes
No

_____

_____

What do you feel is the most important contribution you can make to your health at this time?

_____

_____

Do you feel you have viewed eating as a reward or comfort?
Yes
No

_____

_____

Briefly describe your current daily routine with one of the following:
No set schedule
Partial daily schedule
Whole day planned
Chaotic, but managed
Chaotic and not managed

_____

_____

List three things that you feel needs to change in your daily routine:

_____

_____

_____

How important do you feel God and His Word is to your recovery process?

None

Some

Moderate

Important

Very important

Crucial

All important

_____

_____

What is your level of motivation to follow this program to the end?

No motivation

Very little

Some

Moderate

Much

Highly motivated

_____

_____

_____

**TRUE**
or
**FALSE**

Truth  Meter

Answer the following questions to the best of your ability. Some of these questions may be on the quiz at the end of the Pathway.

1.  In the event of a physical injury, God created our bodies to automatically do what?

_____

2.  What is one of the most important factors in dealing with the inside of a person's body when there is an illness or damage to the body's system?

_____

3.  What kinds of food does God give provision for in Genesis 1:29?

_____

4.  After the flood, God allowed man to eat flesh of animals, or meat. What effect did this have on Man?

_____

5.  Can poor eating habits be considered a life-controlling habit?

    _____

6.  What is the first thing a person must change to change their health through proper nutrition?

    _____

7.  What is the sole purpose for eating?

    _____

8.  What happens to our bodies when we eat harmful foods?

    _____

9.  Since our bodies are made to heal itself, even from the inside, what is the only way to regain complete health?

    _____

10. The body goes through a rebuilding process during what hours?

    _____

11. What is critical that you do during this period?

    _____

12. From about 4am-10am, the body is getting rid of toxins and parasites from the rebuilding process. What is critical that you do not do during this time?

    _____

13. What are three things you should ingest throughout the day to sustain the body's energy requirements?

    _____

    _____

    _____

14. The more raw foods we eat the healthier we will be, because our bodies need the _____ and _____ to rebuild healthy cells.

    _____

    _____

15. When choosing to eat cooked foods, what should you avoid?

    _____

16. Sugar is also very bad for you, what is a good substitute for sugar?

    _____

17. Without proper nutrition, your _____ cannot function as it should

_____

18. Your spiritual health and nutrition is also very important, what does Mathew 4:4 say?

_____

_____

_____

19. What does the Bible say is important concerning our daily routines?

_____

20. What is the most critical element to gaining permanent freedom from your addiction and life-controlling habits?

_____

21. What happens when you have time that is not allocated for something productive?

_____

22. When should you do your program lessons?

_____

23. Before any of your outward behaviors change, what must first take place?

_____

16

**Think about it!**

This area is for writing your thoughts and feelings about the information in this lesson. Please be honest with yourself. This exercise will help you understand and retain what you have read.

Thoughts and Feelings:

_____

_____

_____

_____

_____

_____

_____

_____

_____

_____

_____

Lesson verse: John 17:17

"Sanctify them through thy truth:
thy word is truth."

## Review

This is where the rubber meets the road. You must ask yourself how you will respond to the lesson.

Choose what you believe is the appropriate answer for you, and/or give an explanation of your answer in the space provided. Circle the answer where appropriate.

How important is it to you to know the truth about your addiction problem?
   None
   Somewhat
   Very
   Extremely

_____

_____

How truthful have you been to others about your addiction problem?
   I have tried to completely hide my addiction
   I tell only minor details
   I tell all, but only to certain people
   I have not tried to hide anything

_____

_____

What level of understanding do you feel you have about who God is?
   None
   Little
   Some
   Much

_____

_____

What do you think are the most important kinds of experiences in a person's life?
   Family
   Work related
   Recreational
   Spiritual

_____

_____

TRUE
or
FALSE

Truth ⊙ Meter

Answer the following questions to the best of your ability. Some of these questions may be on the quiz at the end of the Pathway.

18

1. What does the text say is necessary for man to know how to make right decisions?

   _____

2. What is the only method of lasting results in addiction recovery?

   _____

3. What are the four things this lesson mentions that are the fundamentals in understanding addiction behavior?

   _____

   _____

   _____

   _____

4. Making decisions based solely on the emotional desire of the moment, is a good definition of what?

   _____

5. What is the only source of truth? Why?

   _____

   _____

6. After accepting where truth comes from, what is the next step?

   _____

7. The first person we must be truthful with is whom?

   _____

8. What is the only way to lay a proper foundation on which to understand the answer to life-controlling habits?

   _____

**Think about it!**

This area is for writing your thoughts and feelings about the information in this lesson. Please be honest with yourself. This exercise will help you understand and retain what you have read.

Thoughts and Feelings:

_____

_____

_____

_____

_____

_____

_____

_____

_____

_____

Lesson Verse: John 1:17

"For the law was given by Moses, but grace and truth came by Jesus Christ."

## Review

This is where the rubber meets the road. You must ask yourself how you will respond to the lesson.

Choose what you believe is the appropriate answer for you, and/or give an explanation of your answer in the space provided. Circle the answer where appropriate.

What is your current view of authority?

Unnecessary

Overbearing

Totally against you

Helpful

Necessary

_____

_____

Describe what you feel to be your view of God as an authority figure.

_____

_____

Who was the authority figure in your home as a child?

Dad

Mom

Sibling

Uncle/Aunt

_____

_____

How important is it to you to be truthful?

Not

Some

Very

_____

_____

How often do you believe most people are honest?

Hardly ever

Sometimes

Most of the time

Always

_____

_____

TRUE or FALSE

Truth • Meter

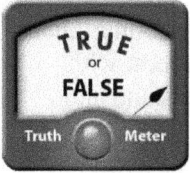

Answer the following questions to the best of your ability. Some of these questions may be on the quiz at the end of the Pathway.

1. The "Laws" that God gave Moses when he was leading the children of Israel across the desert to the land God promised them are called what?

   _____

2. God gives truth to us to maintain what?

   _____

3. What does it mean to "die spiritually"?

   _____

4. What must we do when the laws of man conflict with the laws of God?

   _____

5. God has given man the authority to create laws, these laws should reflect what?

   _____

6. Fill in the blank.
   God's laws are to _____ the development of _____ _____.

   _____

7. Our life has no real meaning or purpose without doing what?

   _____

8. According to the text, what does Genesis 3 give us a record of?

   _____

9. We do not sin because of our environment or circumstances. Why do we sin?

   _____

22

**Think about it!**

This area is for writing your thoughts and feelings about the information in this lesson. Please be honest with yourself. This exercise will help you understand and retain what you have read.

Thoughts and Feelings:

_____

_____

_____

_____

_____

_____

_____

_____

_____

_____

Lesson verse: Jeremiah 17:9

"The heart is deceitful above all things, and desperately wicked: who can know it?"

## Review

This is where the rubber meets the road. You must ask yourself how you will respond to the lesson.

Choose what you believe is the appropriate answer for you, and/or give an explanation of your answer in the space provided. Circle the answer where appropriate.

Do you feel your home environment as a child has affected your life as an adult?
        Yes
        No

_____

_____

Do you believe people are naturally good or bad?
        Good
        Bad

_____

_____

What circumstances as an adult, if any, have influenced your major decisions in life?

_____

_____

How much crime do you believe is a result of social unfairness?
        None
        Some
        Most
        All

_____

_____

What are some decisions you have made that resulted in positive outcomes?

_____

_____

What are some decisions you have made that resulted in negative outcomes?

_____

_____

Answer the following questions to the best of your ability. Some of these questions may be on the quiz at the end of the Pathway.

1. The author states that the heart is what?

_____

2. The secular view of recovery is one in which the addict is cured through _____, and changes in his _____ and _____.

_____

3. The Christian view of recovery is one in which the addict is free from addiction by a change on the _____, or what we would call the _____.

_____

4. This is a supernatural change brought about by God, resulting in what?

_____

5. It is only through _____ the Word of God that we can truly live a _____ and _____ life.

_____

6. Man continues trying to change who he is by changing what?

_____

7. Man's actions and environments are simply a reflection of what?

_____

8. What do certain changes in a person's station in life reveal?

_____

9. To have real freedom from the life-controlling habits that dominate your life now, what is the first important decision that you need to make?

_____

**Think about it!**

This area is for writing your thoughts and feelings about the information in this lesson. Please be honest with yourself. This exercise will help you understand and retain what you have read.

Thoughts and Feelings:

_____

_____

_____

_____

_____

_____

_____

_____

_____

_____

_____

**Lesson verse: Galatians 5:16**

"This I say then, Walk in the Spirit, and ye shall not fulfill the lust of the flesh."

**Review**

This is where the rubber meets the road. You must ask yourself how you will respond to the lesson.

Choose what you believe is the appropriate answer for you, and/or give an explanation of your answer in the space provided. Circle the answer where appropriate.

How important do you think honesty is to our nation's moral character?

None

Some

Very

_____

_____

How honest do you believe you are?

Very little

Some

Mostly

Completely

_____

_____

What part do you believe "religion" plays in honesty?

_____

_____

How important do you think honesty is to our daily activities?

Little

Some

Very

_____

_____

Explain in your own words what you believe "Faith" is.

_____

_____

Do you believe your addiction has played any part in how honest you are as a person?

     Yes

     No

_____

_____

**TRUE or FALSE**
Truth   Meter

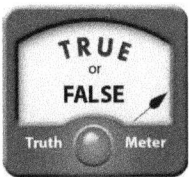

Answer the following questions to the best of your ability. Some of these questions may be on the quiz at the end of the Pathway.

1. According to the text, what is the first challenge to overcome in addiction recovery?

_____

2. What are the three roots of all addictions?

_____

3. What does the author say is a "shallow substitute" for a life God desires them to have?

_____

4. What is the "new life" the author mentions in the text?

_____

5. Once the new life is given, what is given to you next?

_____

6. What is the new nature?

_____

_____

7. What is the only possible way of obtaining the highest level of holiness?

_____

8. Fill in the blank.
     It is on _____ that all other characteristics rest.

_____

9. According to Romans 10:17, How do you attain faith?

_____

10. What does the author say acts as a catalyst for the replacement of normal relationships?

_____

11. When an addict faces the prospect of losing this relationship, what does the author compare it to?

_____

**Think about it!**

This area is for writing your thoughts and feelings about the information in this lesson. Please be honest with yourself. This exercise will help you understand and retain what you have read.

Thoughts and Feelings:

_____
_____
_____
_____
_____
_____
_____
_____
_____
_____
_____
_____

**Lesson verse: Proverbs 29:23**

**"A man's pride shall bring him low; but honor shall uphold the humble in spirit."**

# Review

This is where the rubber meets the road. You must ask yourself how you will respond to the lesson.

Choose what you believe is the appropriate answer for you, and/or give an explanation of your answer in the space provided. Circle the answer where appropriate.

Explain briefly the circumstances surrounding the first time you engaged in addiction activity.

_____

_____

Besides the possible feeling of euphoria or pleasure, were there any feelings of guilt or shame?

Yes

No

_____

_____

Answer the correct type of "Pride" in the following situations.

Wanting to look your best.

Good

Bad

Ignoring advice from a parent.

Good

Bad

Completing a task to the best of your ability.

Good

Bad

Wanting to be admired by others.

Good

Bad

Ignoring the commands of God.

Good

Bad

What do you believe to be the true meaning of humility?

_____

_____

What behaviors in your life have brought about destructive consequences?

_____

_____

TRUE
or
FALSE

Truth  Meter

Answer the following questions to the best of your ability. Some of these questions may be on the quiz at the end of the Pathway.

1. According to Proverbs 29:23, what brings a man low?

_____

2. What is the fundamental basis for every sin that man commits?

_____

3. Every sin is categorized in what three ways?

_____

4. Pride and Selfishness are the root sins of what, which open the door to addiction behavior?

_____

5. The wrong kind of pride is what?

_____

6. According to the definition of Pride in the text, who has the final say in any matter?

_____

7. How are you to discover freedom from life-controlling habits?

_____

8. What does healthy pride reflect?

_____

32

**Think about it!**

This area is for writing your thoughts and feelings about the information in this lesson. Please be honest with yourself. This exercise will help you understand and retain what you have read.

Thoughts and Feelings:

_____

_____

_____

_____

_____

_____

_____

_____

_____

_____

_____

Lesson verse: John 8:32

"And ye shall know the truth, and the truth shall make you free."

## Review

This is where the rubber meets the road. You must ask yourself how you will respond to the lesson.

Choose what you believe is the appropriate answer for you, and/or give an explanation of your answer in the space provided. Circle the answer where appropriate.

33

What circumstances helped you to recognize your need to take an addiction recovery program?

_____

_____

What level of Bible training and knowledge do you feel you have?
   None
   Very little
   Some
   Average
   Much

_____

_____

Describe what you believe to be the definition of "Freedom."

_____

_____

Describe below any feelings of guilt or shame that you have had over your addiction behaviors.

_____

_____

Please tell how you feel about the manner and conditions in which you were reared.

_____

_____

Have you ever experienced a situation of being separated from something or someone you loved?

      Yes

      No

_____

_____

Do you believe God can completely deliver you from your addiction?

      Yes

      No

_____

_____

**TRUE** or **FALSE**

Truth   Meter

Answer the following questions to the best of your ability. Some of these questions may be on the quiz at the end of the Pathway.

1. What is the source for our faith and practice?

_____

2. True freedom from the sin of addiction is found where?

_____

3. What is the secular position that results in false hopes?

_____

_____

4. Why is memorizing Bible verses not humanism?

_____

_____

5. What is the answer to freedom from the bondage of addictions?

_____

6. What do addictions create that controls the mind of the addict?

_____

7. The desire to mask one's reality stems from what?

   _____

8. A feeling of inadequacy is the result of one of what two things?

   _____

9. What is the only way a person can be reconciled to God?

   _____

10. Through confession we find _____, which rests in the forgiveness of sin by Jesus Christ.

   _____

11. What is the source of all power and wisdom?

   _____

# PATHWAY 1 - Review Test

1. Who paid the penalty for sin that God demanded?

_____

2. What has the answers for all things that touch our lives?

_____

3. The recovery process is a lifetime commitment to what?

_____

4. What does the Bible say is important concerning our daily routines?

_____

5. What is the only method of lasting results in addiction recovery?

_____

6. What is the only source of truth? Why?

_____

7. What does it mean to "die spiritually"?

_____

8. Man's actions and environments are simply a reflection of what?

_____

9. What are the three roots of all addictions?

_____

10. Every sin is categorized in what three ways?

_____

11. What is the source for our faith and practice?

_____

12. What is the only way a person can be reconciled to God?

_____

MILSTONE 9

# DOES GOD EXIST?

**Think about it!**

This area is for writing your thoughts and feelings about the information in this lesson. Please be honest with yourself. This exercise will help you understand and retain what you have read.

Thoughts and Feelings:

_____

_____

_____

_____

_____

_____

_____

_____

**Lesson verse: Psalm 14:1**

"The fool hath said in his heart,
There is no God."

## Review

This is where the rubber meets the road. You must ask yourself how you will respond to the lesson.

Choose what you believe is the appropriate answer for you, and/or give an explanation of your answer in the space provided. Circle the answer where appropriate.

38

Do you believe God exists? Why?

    Yes

    No

_____

_____

Describe a situation or action in which your conscience bothered you.

_____

_____

Is there a situation where your conscience helped you make the right decision?

    Yes

    No

_____

_____

Describe some of the ways you believe nature declares the glory of God?

_____

_____

How much do you believe your will has played in your addiction?

    None

    Some

    Much

_____

_____

Why do you believe God wants us to be free from addiction behavior?

_____

_____

Answer the following questions to the best of your ability. Some of these questions may be on the quiz at the end of the Pathway.

39

1. What does the bible call a person who says they do not believe in God?

_____

2. What are the three ways God reveals Himself to us?

_____

3. Why is it important to review how God reveals himself to us?

_____

_____

4. In reference to our conscience, what is already a part of man's nature?

_____

5. What two verses of Scripture support how the Word of God reveals the existence of God?

_____

6. To deny the existence of God is to deny what?

_____

40

**Think about it!**

This area is for writing your thoughts and feelings about the information in this lesson. Please be honest with yourself. This exercise will help you understand and retain what you have read.

Thoughts and Feelings:

_____
_____
_____
_____
_____
_____
_____
_____
_____
_____

**Lesson Verse: Lamentations 3:22-23**

"It is of the LORD's mercies that we are not consumed, because his compassions fail not. They are new every morning: great is thy faithfulness."

## Review

This is where the rubber meets the road. You must ask yourself how you will respond to the lesson.

Choose what you believe is the appropriate answer for you, and/or give an explanation of your answer in the space provided. Circle the answer where appropriate.

What is, or prior to taking this course, what was your belief about who God is?

_____

_____

What does it mean to you to be faithful?

_____

_____

Why do you think it is important to understand the characteristics of God?

_____

_____

**TRUE** or **FALSE**

Truth Meter

Answer the following questions to the best of your ability. Some of these questions may be on the quiz at the end of the Pathway.

1. We cannot hope to be obedient to God's commandments unless we have what?

_____

2. Faithful means _____.

_____

3. According to 1 Chronicles 16:34, how long does God's mercy endure?

_____

4. What Bible verse does the text give showing that God's love is an everlasting love?

_____

5. Living patiently with others is only achievable how?

_____

6. How do the Bible and the text describe God's kindness?

_____

7. Every good and perfect gift comes down from whom?

_____

8. To surrender means that you must _____

_____

**Think about it!**

This area is for writing your thoughts and feelings about the information in this lesson. Please be honest with yourself. This exercise will help you understand and retain what you have read.

43

## Thoughts and Feelings:

_____
_____
_____
_____
_____
_____
_____
_____
_____
_____
_____

**Lesson verse: Romans 11:33**

"O the depth of the riches both of the wisdom and knowledge of God! how unsearchable are his judgments, and his ways past finding out!"

## Review

Choose what you believe is the appropriate answer for you, and/or give an explanation of your answer in the space provided. Circle the answer where appropriate.

44

Prior to starting this course, what do you believe your level of relationship was with God?

None

Some

Strong

_____

_____

How important do you believe is having a purpose for life?

None

Some

Very

_____

_____

Do you believe you have a specific purpose in life? If yes, what is that purpose? If not, why?

Yes

No

_____

_____

What does it mean to be selfish?

_____

_____

Why do you believe God wants us to be giving toward others?

_____

_____

Answer the following questions to the best of your ability. Some of these questions may be on the quiz at the end of the Pathway.

1. God created man as a _____

   _____

2. According to Hebrews 11:6, how do we please God?

   _____

3. What produces faith according to the text?

   _____

4. We were created to what?

   _____

5. God resists the proud and gives what to the humble?

   _____

6. Selfishness and Pride are catalysts for what?

   _____

7. Religion only satisfies _____.

   _____

8. What can God NOT do, according to Titus 1:2?

   _____

9. What gives us a clear presentation of the concept of God?

   _____

10. "God is a Spirit: and they that worship him must worship him in spirit and in truth." Where is this found in the Bible?

    _____

11. What is the most important way in which God deals with us?

    _____

46

**Think about it!**

This area is for writing your thoughts and feelings about the information in this lesson. Please be honest with yourself. This exercise will help you understand and retain what you have read.

Thoughts and Feelings:

_____

_____

_____

_____

_____

_____

_____

_____

_____

_____

_____

Lesson verse: Isaiah 6:3,

"And one cried unto another, and said, Holy, holy, holy, is the LORD of hosts: the whole earth is full of his glory."

# Review

This is where the rubber meets the road. You must ask yourself how you will respond to the lesson.

Choose what you believe is the appropriate answer for you, and/or give an explanation of your answer in the space provided. Circle the answer where appropriate.

Prior to starting this course, what level of understanding did you have about sin? Explain.

No understanding
Some understanding
Clear understanding

_____

_____


How do you feel sin and addictions relate to one another?

_____

_____


Explain why it should matter to you how God sees addiction.

_____

_____


Describe how your view of how God sees addiction may have changed as a result of this course so far.

_____

_____


Try and explain how the characteristics of God relate to our relationship with Him.

_____

_____


At what level do you believe God wants us to trust Him?

None
Some
Completely

_____

_____

Why is just being free from addiction not sufficient for you to fellowship with God?

_____

_____

**TRUE**
or
**FALSE**

Truth    Meter

Answer the following questions to the best of your ability. Some of these questions may be on the quiz at the end of the Pathway.

1. The Bible describes the root problem of the manifestations of addictions as _____.

_____

2. When does God give us the desire to please Him?

_____

3. How is a person, that spends their waking hours with things that distract them from the reminder that they are not right with God, described in the text

_____

4. What is to be our guide?

_____

5. Why is it is critical that a person begin following Christ in obedience to God's Word early in life?

_____

6. God hates _____.

_____

7. Proverbs 3:5-7 says we are to not lean on what?

_____

8. What does it mean to be Holy?

_____

9. "Holy, holy, holy" means what according to the text?

   _____

10. The goal of addiction recovery is:

   _____

50

**Think about it!**

This area is for writing your thoughts and feelings about the information in this lesson. Please be honest with yourself. This exercise will help you understand and retain what you have read.

Thoughts and Feelings:

_____

_____

_____

_____

_____

_____

_____

_____

_____

_____

**Lesson Verse: Romans 6:22**

"But now being made free from sin, and become servants to God, ye have your fruit unto holiness, and the end everlasting life.

## Review

This is where the rubber meets the road. You must ask yourself how you will respond to the lesson.

Choose what you believe is the appropriate answer for you, and/or give an explanation of your answer in the space provided. Circle the answer where appropriate.

Describe some expectations you have had for other people in your life.

_____

_____

Explain your belief or concept of Hell.

_____

_____

Explain your belief or concept of Heaven.

_____

_____

Explain what you believe to be your purpose for having been created.

_____

_____

At this point in the course, explain your concept of salvation.

_____

_____

What are some talents that you feel God has given you?

_____

_____

Describe what you believe God wants you to do with the talents He has given you.

_____

_____

Answer the following questions to the best of your ability. Some of these questions may be on the quiz at the end of the Pathway.

1. What command has God given us in Exodus 20?

   _____

2. What is an idol?

   _____

3. Addiction is simply _____ .

   _____

4. Romans 6:23 says that the wages of sin is _____ .

   _____

5. What is the gift of God according to the same passage?

   _____

6. What does a person have to do to avoid eternal separation from God, in Hell?

   _____

7. What does God require for us to be with Him in Heaven?

   _____

8. How can our sins be forgiven?

   _____

   _____

# GOD'S PLAN OF SALVATION

**Think about it!**

This area is for writing your thoughts and feelings about the information in this lesson. Please be honest with yourself. This exercise will help you understand and retain what you have read.

Thoughts and Feelings:

_____

_____

_____

_____

_____

_____

_____

_____

_____

_____

_____

**Lesson verse: John 14:6**

**"Jesus saith unto him, I am the way, the truth, and the life: no man cometh unto the Father, but by me."**

## Review

Choose what you believe is the appropriate answer for you, and/or give an explanation of your answer in the space provided. Circle the answer where appropriate.

54

Describe some expectations you have had for other people in your life.

_____

_____

Explain your belief or concept of "evidences of salvation."

_____

_____

Explain your belief or concept of "fellowship with God."

_____

_____

Explain what you believe to be your purpose for having been created.

_____

_____

At this point in the course, explain your concept of "sanctification."

_____

_____

What are some blessings that you feel God has already given to you?

_____

_____

Describe why you believe God has given you these blessings.

_____

_____

**TRUE** or **FALSE** — Truth Meter

Answer the following questions to the best of your ability. Some of these questions may be on the quiz at the end of the Pathway.

1. By who does John 14:6 says we go in order to come before the Father?

   _____

2. What are the 7 parts of the Plan of Salvation

   All men are sinners
   Sin must be paid for
   Death is the penalty for sin

   _____

   God provided us a payment
   Jesus Christ, God's Son, paid our sin debt for us, as us on Calvary

   _____

3. What is the most obvious evidence of a believer

   _____

4. What is a process where God sets believers apart as holy servants for His purposes?

   _____

5. Hebrews 4:14-16 says can come boldly before God's throne and obtain _____ and find _____.

   _____

6. According to Proverbs 3:5-6, how does God direct our paths?

   _____

7. A meaningful relationship with God is only accomplished how?

   _____

8. It is only through a _____ that a person can gain lasting recovery from the bondage of addiction.

   _____

9. Obedience to Christ gives us what from God?

   _____

10. It is impossible to live free from addictions without what?

_____

11. According to Romans 14:12, we are to be _____ for our life?

_____

# MILSTONE 15

# GOD'S PLAN FOR MAN



**Think about it!**

This area is for writing your thoughts and feelings about the information in this lesson. Please be honest with yourself. This exercise will help you understand and retain what you have read.

Thoughts and Feelings:

**Lesson Verse: Proverbs 3:5-6**

**"Trust in the LORD with all thine heart; and lean not unto thine own understanding. In all thy ways acknowledge him, and he shall direct thy paths."**

**Review**

This is where the rubber meets the road. You must ask yourself how you will respond to the lesson.

Choose what you believe is the appropriate answer for you, and/or give an explanation of your answer in the space provided. Circle the answer where appropriate.

Describe several situations where you had to rely on someone else for help.

_____

_____

Think about and write what you believe to be benefits of placing our trust in God.

_____

_____

Describe, what you believe to be, some "cares" you can place on God.

_____

_____

How important do you believe church attendance to be in your life? Why?
None
Some
Very

_____

_____

How important do you believe us fellowshipping with God is to Him?
None
Some
Very

_____

_____

Answer the following questions to the best of your ability. Some of these questions may be on the quiz at the end of the Pathway.

1. Adam and Eve fellowshipped with God until what?

   _____

2. Proverbs 3:5 says that we are to trust in the Lord how?

   _____

3. With how much does God want us to trust Him?

   _____

4. What will we have if know the outcome of our life is in God's hands?

   _____

5. 1 Peter 5:7 says what?

   _____

6. The text describes addiction as what?

   _____

7. Where do we find God's commands?

   _____

8. Truth comes from _____.

   _____

9. What is God's ultimate plan for man

   _____

10. Christ is our _____.

   _____

# PATHWAY 2 - Review Test

1. What does the bible refer to a person who says they do not believe in God?

_____

2. We cannot hope to be obedient to God's commandments unless we have what?

_____

3. Selfishness and Pride are catalysts for what?

_____

4. Proverbs 3:5-7 says we are to not lean on what?

_____

5. What is an idol?

_____

6. How can our sins be forgiven?

_____

7. It is impossible to live free from addictions without what?

_____

8. Truth comes from _____.

_____

9. Adam and Eve fellowshipped with God until what?

_____

10. A meaningful relationship with God is only accomplished how?

_____

**Think about it!**

This area is for writing your thoughts and feelings about the information in this lesson. Please be honest with yourself. This exercise will help you understand and retain what you have read.

Thoughts and Feelings:

_____

_____

_____

_____

_____

_____

_____

Lesson Verse: 2 Timothy 3:13

"But evil men and seducers shall wax worse and worse, deceiving, and being deceived."

**Review**

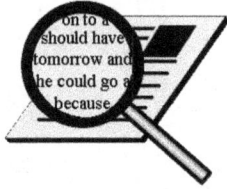

This is where the rubber meets the road. You must ask yourself how you will respond to the lesson.

Choose what you believe is the appropriate answer for you, and/or give an explanation of your answer in the space provided. Circle the answer where appropriate.

What has influenced your thinking, more than anything else, about from where man came?

Home

School

Church

Television

Society

_____

_____

Name some sources in your life that may have taught you that life has no meaning or value.

_____

_____

Why do you believe Satan has tried to substitute good things that God has created?

_____

_____

Explain some ways in which you believe God made man like Himself.

_____

_____

Describe some ways in which you see man as being "broken."

_____

_____

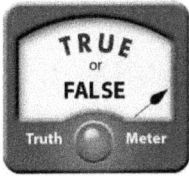

Answer the following questions to the best of your ability. Some of these questions may be on the quiz at the end of the Pathway.

Please answer the following questions to the best of your ability. Write your answers in the spaces provided.

1. Man is not _____ _____ as some people believe.

2. Our society today is teaching people that they have no real _____ __ _____, either personally or otherwise.

3. The absence of _____ ___ _____ in life is also reflected in the way some individuals mutilate, pierce, and tattoo their bodies.

4. Each person is valuable to God because He not only created them, but because He gave His ____ _____ ___ to die for their sins.

5. The murdering of innocent, unborn lives is a reflection of the _____ ___ _____ of the perceived value of life itself.

6. There is an absence of purpose and value in the societies of our world because Satan has attempted to replace God and creation with _____ ___ _____.

7. God teaches us in His Word that man was created as a _____ ___ _____ _____ being.

8. Because God created man, God has the answer to _____ _____ and any other problem man may have in his life.

9. The complexities and intricacies of the world in which we exist scream out the truth that all things were created with a definite _____ ___ _____.

64

**Think about it!**

This area is for writing your thoughts and feelings about the information in this lesson. Please be honest with yourself. This exercise will help you understand and retain what you have read.

Thoughts and Feelings:

_____
_____
_____
_____
_____
_____
_____
_____
_____
_____
_____

**Lesson verse: Ecclesiastes 12:13**

"Let us hear the conclusion of the whole matter: Fear God, and keep his commandments: for this is the whole duty of man."

# Review

This is where the rubber meets the road. You must ask yourself how you will respond to the lesson.

Choose what you believe is the appropriate answer for you, and/or give an explanation of your answer in the space provided. Circle the answer where appropriate.

What are some responsibilities that we have as adults that we did not have as adolescents?

_____

_____

In what ways should people reflect the characteristics of God?

_____

_____

What do you feel is your level of obedience to God at this moment in your life? Explain.

    None

    Very little

    Some

    High

_____

_____

Describe ways in which we can have a relationship with God.

_____

_____

Explain what it means to have a fear of God.

_____

_____

What are some ways that we can show that we have a correct fear of God?

_____

_____

Describe some ways in which God shows His love for us.

_____

_____

Give a specific way that God has shown His love for you.

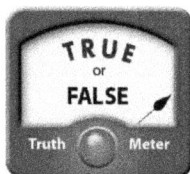

_____

_____

Answer the following questions to the best of your ability. Some of these questions may be on the quiz at the end of the Pathway.

Please answer the following questions to the best of your ability. Write your answers in the spaces provided.

1. Because we are created in the image and likeness of God, our basic responsibility is to reflect the _____ of the Creator.

2. Our purpose in life can become clouded by our _____ _____ to God.

3. Our primary responsibility toward God is to reflect His nature and to fulfill the _____ for which we are created.

4. God tells us in several different places in Scripture that wisdom begins with _____ ____.

5. _____ _____ _____ is the real evidence of whether or not we truly love God.

6. When we honestly begin to understand just how much God loves us, we can't help but respond by _____ ___ in return.

**Think about it!**

This area is for writing your thoughts and feelings about the information in this lesson. Please be honest with yourself. This exercise will help you understand and retain what you have read.

## Thoughts and Feelings:

_____

_____

_____

_____

_____

_____

_____

_____

_____

_____

_____

**Lesson verse: Psalm 8:4**

"What is man, that thou art mindful of him? And the son of man that thou visitest him?"

## Review

This is where the rubber meets the road. You must ask yourself how you will respond to the lesson.

Choose what you believe is the appropriate answer for you, and/or give an explanation of your answer in the space provided. Circle the answer where appropriate.

What measure do you feel have been the majority of choices you have made in life?
Poor
Fair
Good
Excellent

_____

_____

In what ways have you become a product of the choices you have made in life?

_____

_____

Describe the kind of activities and behaviors that have been the result of poor choices in your life.

_____

_____

Describe the kind of activities and behaviors that have been the result of good choices in your life.

_____

_____

TRUE or FALSE
Truth Meter

Answer the following questions to the best of your ability. Some of these questions may be on the quiz at the end of the Pathway.

Please answer the following questions to the best of your ability. Write your answers in the spaces provided.

1. Man has a responsibility to _____ ____ with the mind and body He gave us.

2. As Christ lives both in and through a person, that person becomes more and more _____ to God and His laws.

3. When people ____ _____ for their choices, all they are doing is denying their responsibility for their behavior.

4. Once a person reaches a certain age they become the _____ of the choices they make in life, not a _____ of circumstances.

5. Before we can understand how addictions take such a strong hold on someone's life, we must understand why people make ____ ___ ___ _____.

6. Once the addict's habits are formed, it is not as much a result of the will of the addict that makes him continue, but rather the _____ __ ___ ____ to the behavior.

7. We act or behave in response to what we _____ _____ _____ in relation to God.

8. Understanding how God views us and what we believe about God in return, dictates ___ _____ in any given circumstance.

9. What we believe about God is another reflection of what we were taught in our _____ _____ as a child.

10. We must first understand who God is before we can understand what it is He wants us to do and ___ __ ___ __ ____.

70

**Think about it!**

This area is for writing your thoughts and feelings about the information in this lesson. Please be honest with yourself. This exercise will help you understand and retain what you have read.

Thoughts and Feelings:

_____

_____

_____

_____

_____

_____

_____

_____

_____

_____

_____

**Lesson Verse: Isaiah 45:12**

"I have made the earth, and created man upon it: I, *even* my hands, have stretched out the heavens, and all their host have I commanded."

## Review

This is where the rubber meets the road. You must ask yourself how you will respond to the lesson.

Choose what you believe is the appropriate answer for you, and/or give an explanation of your answer in the space provided. Circle the answer where appropriate.

71

Describe some of the things in nature that reveal the creative power of God.

_____

_____

What are some things about our body that reveal the creative power of God?

_____

_____

Name some things you can do that would have a positive effect on your Body.

_____

_____

**TRUE** or **FALSE**

Truth   Meter

Answer the following questions to the best of your ability. Some of these questions may be on the quiz at the end of the Pathway.

Please answer the following questions to the best of your ability. Write your answers in the spaces provided.

1. There are evidences we find in nature that reveal the _____ _____ of God.

2. _____ does not and cannot result from disorder.

3. There must be a _____ _____ for our complex world to exist.

4. Even though Satan has been very successful at this substitute, it does not change the reality that man is still _____ __ ___ _____ ____ and will someday stand before Him in judgment.

5. Because Satan has created _____ for God's many wonderful gifts to mankind, we must be careful to recognize the difference.

6. The most dangerous lie is the lie that is _____ __ ___ _____.

7. The ability to recognize truth from error is called _____.

8. Discernment comes from _____ ___ _____ the Word of God, and allowing the Holy Spirit of God to teach us.

**Think about it!**

This area is for writing your thoughts and feelings about the information in this lesson. Please be honest with yourself. This exercise will help you understand and retain what you have read.

73

## Thoughts and Feelings:

_____

_____

_____

_____

_____

_____

_____

_____

_____

_____

_____

**Lesson Verse: Genesis 1:1,2**

"And God said, Let the earth bring forth grass, the herb yielding seed, and the fruit tree yielding fruit after his kind, whose seed is in itself, upon the earth: and it was so."

**Review**

74

This is where the rubber meets the road. You must ask yourself how you will respond to the lesson.

Choose what you believe is the appropriate answer for you, and/or give an explanation of your answer in the space provided. Circle the answer where appropriate.

What level of effect do you believe marijuana use has on a person's body and mind? Explain.

None

Very little

Some

Great

_____

_____

How does marijuana use reveal the true nature of man?

_____

_____

Explain how marijuana use reflects man's lack of understanding of the meaning of life.

_____

_____

**TRUE** or **FALSE**

Truth ◉ Meter

Answer the following questions to the best of your ability. Some of these questions may be on the quiz at the end of the Pathway.

Please answer the following questions to the best of your ability. Write your answers in the spaces provided.

1. Marijuana is one of the most useful _____ in all of God's creation.

2. The plant that the drug called THC comes from is called _____ or Hemp.

3. The _____ of the hemp plant is an ideal material to make fiber board, paper, and other construction products.

4. To accuse God of making an error in creating substances that can be misused would leave God with _____ __ _____.

5. The hemp plant has the potential for _____ _____.

6. What we need to do is to convince people to treat their bodies with respect and care since it is the _____ __ ___.

76

**Think about it!**

This area is for writing your thoughts and feelings about the information in this lesson. Please be honest with yourself. This exercise will help you understand and retain what you have read.

Thoughts and Feelings:

_____

_____

_____

_____

_____

_____

_____

_____

_____

_____

**Lesson Verse: Genesis 1:27**

"So God created man in his own image, in the image of God created he him; male and female created he them."

## Review

This is where the rubber meets the road. You must ask yourself how you will respond to the lesson.

Choose what you believe is the appropriate answer for you, and/or give an explanation of your answer in the space provided. Circle the answer where appropriate.

Explain in what ways obedience to God can bring fulfillment to a person.

_____

_____

What level of value and significance do you believe man has to God? Why?
None
Very little
Some
Much

_____

_____

Describe actions of our society in general that show how wicked the heart of man is.

_____

_____

How would you describe your own heart and actions?
Wicked
Poor
Average
Pure

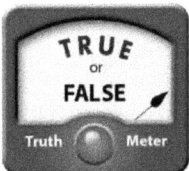

_____

_____

**TRUE** or **FALSE**

Truth Meter

Answer the following questions to the best of your ability. Some of these questions may be on the quiz at the end of the Pathway.

Please answer the following questions to the best of your ability. Write your answers in the spaces provided.

1. There can be no mistaking the fact that God is the _____ and that He created humanity as well as all things.

2. Because man was made in _____ _____, and created with a specific purpose, man is also accountable to Him and must obey the laws of God.

3. For man to, not fulfill the purpose for which he was created, is to _____ __ _____ this value and significance.

4. Being created in God's image gives the life of every human being very personal _____ ___ _____.

5. Because we were made in the _____ __ ___ _____, our lives have both value and significance.

6. Man is definitely not a product of his _____.

7. You must choose to believe that God created all things for His glory and for our _____.

# PATHWAY 3 - Review Test

1. Because we are created in the image and likeness of God, our basic responsibility is to reflect the _____ of the Creator.

   _____

2. God tells us in several different places in Scripture that wisdom begins with _____ ___.

   _____

3. We act or behave in response to what we _____ _____ _____ in relation to God.

   _____

4. What we believe about God is another reflection of what we were taught in our _____ _____ as a child.

   _____

5. There are evidences we find in nature that reveal the _____ _____ of God.

   _____

6. The most dangerous lie is the lie that is _____ __ ___ _____.

   _____

7. The ability to recognize truth from error is called _____.

   _____

8. To accuse God of making an error in creating substances that can be misused would leave God with _____ __ _____.

   _____

9. Being created in God's image gives the life of every human being very personal _____ ___ _____.

   _____

# PATHWAY 4
# PURPOSE

## MILSTONE 22
## PURPOSE AND SIGNIFICANCE

**Think about it!**

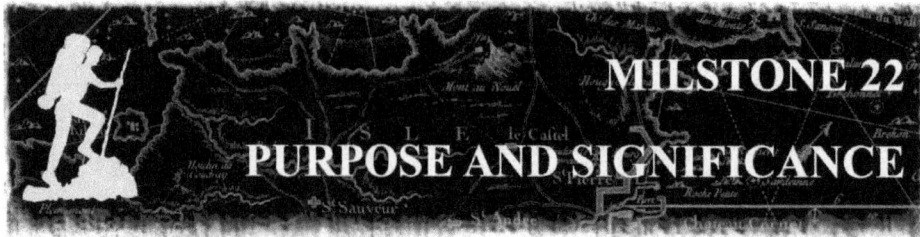

This area is for writing your thoughts and feelings about the information in this lesson. Please be honest with yourself. This exercise will help you understand and retain what you have read.

Thoughts and Feelings:

_____
_____
_____
_____
_____
_____

Lesson Verse: Ephesians 3:11

"According to the eternal purpose which he purposed in Christ Jesus our Lord."

## Review

This is where the rubber meets the road. You must ask yourself how you will respond to the lesson.

Choose what you believe is the appropriate answer for you, and/or give an explanation of your answer in the space provided. Circle the answer where appropriate.

How important to you is having a purpose in life? Why?
None
Some
Very

_____

_____

Describe a situation or event where you felt it was necessary to make a "tradeoff."

_____

_____

In what ways, in the past, have you felt yourself being rebellious toward authority?

_____

_____

Explain what you believe to be the definition of significance.

_____

_____

At this moment, how significant do you feel you are to God? Why?
None
Some
Very

_____

_____

TRUE
or
FALSE

Truth    Meter

Answer the following questions to the best of your ability. Some of these questions may be on the quiz at the end of the Pathway.

Please answer the following questions to the best of your ability. Write your answers in the spaces provided.

1. Before we can know ___ _____ __ ____ _____, we must understand what God says about our purpose.

2. Many people are trying to find purpose for their _____.

3. God did not create this _____ ___ _____ without having a purpose for doing so.

4. The reason God has given to all men purpose is _____ _____.

5. Jesus Christ is the reason as well as the _____ of purpose and significance.

6. The definition of _____ is "meaning or importance."

7. Christ alone must be the _____ __ _____ for the right purpose in life to exist.

8. Man possesses an _____ _____ of the Creator.

9. The choice to accept God's truth regarding purpose and significance leads to a life filled with ___ ___ _____.

**Think about it!**

This area is for writing your thoughts and feelings about the information in this lesson. Please be honest with yourself. This exercise will help you understand and retain what you have read.

Thoughts and Feelings:

_____

_____

_____

_____

_____

_____

_____

_____

_____

_____

_____

_____

**Lesson Verse: 2Timothy 1:9**

"Who hath saved us, and called us with an holy calling, not according to our works, but according to his own purpose and grace, which was given us in Christ Jesus before the world began,"

**Review**

84

This is where the rubber meets the road. You must ask yourself how you will respond to the lesson.

Choose what you believe is the appropriate answer for you, and/or give an explanation of your answer in the space provided. Circle the answer where appropriate.

What do you believe to be your reason for living?

_____

_____

What would you choose to be the singleness of purpose for your life?

_____

_____

Describe what you believe to be God's purpose for creating mankind.

_____

_____

What does it mean to you to, "Give God His rightful place in your life?"

_____

_____

Explain in your own words what it means to have a relationship with God.

_____

_____

TRUE
or
FALSE

Truth    Meter

Answer the following questions to the best of your ability. Some of these questions may be on the quiz at the end of the Pathway.

Please answer the following questions to the best of your ability. Write your answers in the spaces provided.

1. The world's key motivation for _____ ___ _____ in this world is to have a purpose for which to exist.

2. God must have His _____ _____ in men's hearts and lives.

3. Purpose begins with _____ _____ in the world.

4. Purpose for life begins_____ _____, not before.

5. The meaning of life is God _____ __ __ _____.

6. We are here to ____ ___, not to accomplish some great work or live for self-gain.

7. The greatest _____ we could ever have is coming to know the Lord.

8. The will of God is _____ in the Bible.

9. When man lives _____ of God's purpose, he is empty and discontented.

10. It is the will of God that all men _____ _____ by accepting Jesus Christ as their personal Saviour.

86

**Think about it!**

This area is for writing your thoughts and feelings about the information in this lesson. Please be honest with yourself. This exercise will help you understand and retain what you have read.

Thoughts and Feelings:

_____
_____
_____
_____
_____
_____
_____
_____
_____
_____
_____

**Lesson Verse: 1Corinthians 10:31**

"Whether therefore ye eat, or drink, or whatsoever ye do, do all to the glory of God."

## Review

This is where the rubber meets the road. You must ask yourself how you will respond to the lesson.

Choose what you believe is the appropriate answer for you, and/or give an explanation of your answer in the space provided. Circle the answer where appropriate.

Describe your idea of who you thought God was when you were a teenager.

_____

_____

Give some circumstances where you were influenced by peer pressures.

_____

_____

How did your response to this peer pressure affect your life? Explain why.
   None
   Positively
   Negatively

_____

_____

How much exposure to the Bible did you have growing up as a child?
   None
   Occasional
   Some
   Much

_____

_____

Have you ever been identified with a particular group of people? If yes, explain.
   Yes
   No

_____

_____

If you answered yes to the above question, how did being a part of that group make you feel?

a. _____

_____

Do you know anyone who has lost their life as a result of addiction activity? Explain.

Yes

No

_____

_____

TRUE
or
FALSE

Truth     Meter

Answer the following questions to the best of your ability. Some of these questions may be on the quiz at the end of the Pathway.

Please answer the following questions to the best of your ability. Write your answers in the spaces provided.

1. The strongest forces in people's lives are usually _____ _____.

2. The clear purpose of man is to _____ _____ to God.

3. Because God created man __ ___ _____, man's life has sanctity, value, and significance to Him as the Creator.

4. There is no ____ ___ to be a follower of Christ.

5. Since we know that no man is good, according to Romans 3: 10, the only way a man can be good is to __ __ _____ or to have received Christ as his Saviour.

6. People who have _____ _____ __ _____ _____ have a plan for his or her life that God has already established.

**Think about it!**

This area is for writing your thoughts and feelings about the information in this lesson. Please be honest with yourself. This exercise will help you understand and retain what you have read.

89

Thoughts and Feelings:

_____

_____

_____

_____

_____

_____

_____

_____

_____

_____

_____

**Lesson Verse: Philippians 4:13**

**"I can do all things through Christ, which strengtheneth me."**

**Review**

This is where the rubber meets the road. You must ask yourself how you will respond to the lesson.

Choose what you believe is the appropriate answer for you, and/or give an explanation of your answer in the space provided. Circle the answer where appropriate.

What has been the dominating object of your affections? Explain.
    Your addiction
    A person
    A sport
    A cause

_____

_____

What have you always believed to be the cause of your addiction?
    You
    Circumstances
    Friends
    Curiosity

_____

_____

Do you feel you have damaged the trust people have for you?
    Yes
    No

_____

_____

Tell about any person who has stood by you during your addiction problems.

_____

_____

What does it mean to you to have a person stand by you, regardless of your situation?

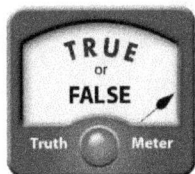

_____

_____

TRUE
or
FALSE

Truth    Meter

91

Answer the following questions to the best of your ability. Some of these questions may be on the quiz at the end of the Pathway.

Please answer the following questions to the best of your ability. Write your answers in the spaces provided.

1. As we ____ __ _____ and our relationship becomes stronger, we see and hear more and more of His voice leading us and guiding us.

2. When we place our trust in God, the outcome becomes ___ _____.

3. When a person accepts Christ for the forgiveness of their sins, and begins walking this path of obedience, ____ ___ ____ increases over time.

4. When God becomes the _____ __ _ _____ _____, it gives that person the motivation to do things that are pleasing to God and not things that are pleasing to self.

5. It is important to believe that God can, and will, _____ ___, if a person will ask God for forgiveness.

6. A person who has struggled with addiction must be devoted to _____ ____ ____ ___ in order to be free from the addiction and fear of relapse.

7. It takes a very long time to _____ _____ that has been destroyed through the activities associated with life-controlling habits.

8. Regardless of the past, living a Christian life is the ____ ____ a person can live on this earth.

92

**Think about it!**

This area is for writing your thoughts and feelings about the information in this lesson. Please be honest with yourself. This exercise will help you understand and retain what you have read.

Thoughts and Feelings:

_____

_____

_____

_____

_____

_____

_____

_____

_____

_____

_____

**Lesson Verse: John 3:16**

"For God so loved the world, that he gave his only begotten Son, that whosoever believeth in him should not perish, but have everlasting life."

## Review

This is where the rubber meets the road. You must ask yourself how you will respond to the lesson.

Choose what you believe is the appropriate answer for you, and/or give an explanation of your answer in the space provided. Circle the answer where appropriate.

Describe some of the consequences you have endured as a result of your addiction.

_____

_____

_____

How many other people do you know that are struggling with life-controlling habits and behaviors?

Less than 5

Between 5 and 10

More than 10

More than 30

Describe how you felt about addiction problems before your own addiction began.

_____

_____

How many relationships do you believe have been damaged as a result of your addiction?

None

1 to 5

5 to 10

More than 10

_____

_____

How strongly do you feel your addiction has a hold on you?

None

Very little

Some

Extreme

_____

_____

How often have you attended church in the past?
Never
Occasionally
On holidays
Every week

TRUE
or
FALSE

Truth   Meter

Answer the following questions to the best of your ability.
Some of these questions may be on the quiz at the end of the
Pathway.

Please answer the following questions to the best of your ability. Write your answers in the
spaces provided.

1. Addictions result in very serious, and many times terrible, _____ in the lives
   of addicts and their loved ones.

2. Addictions take a terrible toll on ___ _____ and society.

3. Addictions _____ from our society people who would otherwise be _____.

4. _____ ____ are laws that God established that are given to us for instruction, and
   pertain to the actions of any person, regardless of race, religion, or gender.

5. The _____ and _____ alike are accountable to these natural laws.

6. A literal burning hell awaits all those who _____ _____ _____ as their Saviour.

7. Men worship themselves (the creature) through _____, and continue
   to disbelieve anything negative will happen to them.

8. Addictions may only appear to affect a small percentage of our society, but in truth
   have very _____ consequences.

9. When there is no foundation or objective standard by which people make decisions for their life, they make decisions based solely on the _____ _____ of the moment.

10. When society is in decay from the _____ __ ____, significance is hidden from the minds of men.

11. Nothing has value or _____ in a culture where anything goes.

12. You must realize that life-controlling habits and behaviors ____ __ _____ from you that you are already significant to God.

96

**Think about it!**

This area is for writing your thoughts and feelings about the information in this lesson. Please be honest with yourself. This exercise will help you understand and retain what you have read.

Thoughts and Feelings:

_____

_____

_____

_____

_____

_____

_____

_____

_____

_____

_____

**Lesson Verse: Romans 1:16**

"For I am not ashamed of the gospel of Christ; for it is the power of God unto salvation, to every one that believeth..."

## Review

This is where the rubber meets the road. You must ask yourself how you will respond to the lesson.

Choose what you believe is the appropriate answer for you, and/or give an explanation of your answer in the space provided. Circle the answer where appropriate.

Describe the kind of influences you have had in your lifetime.
Poor
Average
Good

_____

_____

Tell about a person you have known that demonstrated the love of God toward you.

_____

_____

How often do you worry about relapse?
Never
Seldom
Frequently
Most of the time

_____

_____

Explain your definition of surrender.

_____

_____

What do you believe is meant by the statement, "you must surrender to God?"

_____

_____

Answer the following questions to the best of your ability. Some of these questions may be on the quiz at the end of the Pathway.

Please answer the following questions to the best of your ability. Write your answers in the spaces provided.

1. It is impossible to have any kind of meaningful relationship with a person without _____ _____ with them.

2. As a young couple learns more about one another, over time, their friendship and commitment turn into _____ ___ _____ for one another.

3. Understanding our _____ __ ____ may not be learned at an early age for some people, but it can still be learned at any age.

4. The love of Christ demonstrated in the life of a Believer is one of the best ways to convey the truth to others that ___ __ ____.

5. It is the responsibility of the ____ _____ to convict a person of sin and draw them to God.

6. Giving the _____ __ _____ to you is the main purpose of this addiction recovery ministry.

7. When a person realizes in their heart that they should and want to please God, they will adjust their _____ accordingly.

8. As spiritual things become more _____ in the life of a Christian, there are fewer things in their life that are _____ to God.

9. The process of _____ brings about an understanding of the true purpose in life.

10. Learning how to _____ __ ___ and His will for your life is a part of the process of sanctification.

# PATHWAY 4 - Review Test

1. Jesus Christ is the reason as well as the _____ of purpose and significance.

   _____

2. Christ alone must be the _____ __ _____ for the right purpose in life to exist.

   _____

3. Purpose for life begins_____ _____, not before.

   _____

4. The meaning of life is God _____ __ __ _____.

   _____

5. The greatest _____ we could ever have is coming to know the Lord.

   _____

6. The clear purpose of man is to _____ _____ to God.

   _____

7. When we place our trust in God, the outcome becomes ___ _____.

   _____

8. Regardless of the past, living a Christian life is the ____ ____ a person can live on this earth.

   _____

9. Addictions _____ from our society people who would otherwise be _____.

   _____

10. When society is in decay from the _____ __ ___, significance is hidden from the minds of men.

   _____

# PATHWAY 5
# ACCOUNTABILITY

## MILSTONE 28
## ORIGINS OF ACCOUNTABILITY

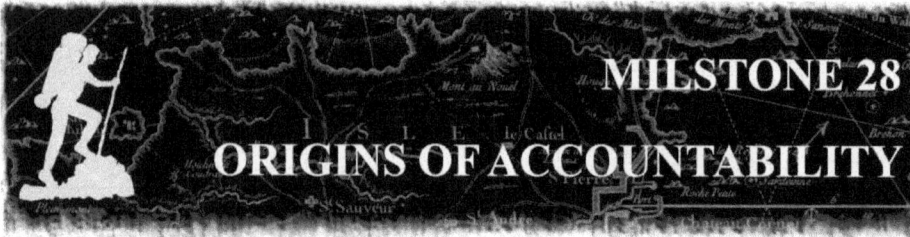

**Think about it!**

This area is for writing your thoughts and feelings about the information in this lesson. Please be honest with yourself. This exercise will help you understand and retain what you have read.

Thoughts and Feelings:

_____

_____

_____

_____

_____

_____

**Lesson Verse: Ecclesiastes 12:13-14**

"Let us hear the conclusion of the whole matter: Fear God, and keep his commandments: for this is the whole duty of man."

**Review**

This is where the rubber meets the road. You must ask yourself how you will respond to the lesson.

Choose what you believe is the appropriate answer for you, and/or give an explanation of your answer in the space provided. Circle the answer where appropriate.

Describe a situation where you felt you were all alone.

_____

_____

Give your definition of accountability.

_____

_____

In what ways have your addiction affected people that are the closest to you?

_____

_____

Name someone who you admire and look up to. Why?

_____

_____

_____

Describe the qualities of someone you believe should be a role model to others.

_____

_____

**TRUE** or **FALSE**

Truth Meter

Answer the following questions to the best of your ability. Some of these questions may be on the quiz at the end of the Pathway.

Please answer the following questions to the best of your ability. Write your answers in the spaces provided.

1. The reason we deal with accountability and relationships is to help people understand their accountability toward ___ ___ ___ and how their conduct and behavior are affected or _____ by their motives.

2. If we have lived in obedience to God's Word, when we stand before Him at the judgment, our works will have been of His will and _____, our lives of His _____, and our relationships of his _____.

3. It has often been said, "No man is an island."‖ We use this quote many times to illustrate man's _____ to one another.

4. God told Adam and Eve to be _____ ___ _____.

5. Adam and Eve did not consider the results of their _____ of accountability.

6. Adam and Eve's decision to disobey God gave their children a ____ _____ to follow.

7. Understanding our accountability to ___ _____, and then to our fellow man, allows us to recognize our need of living in obedience to God's commands.

8. It is _____ _____ that we recognize our accountability toward Him and that we obey Him.

9. We must submit our will to God and allow Him to have control of our _____ and our _____.

**Think about it!**

This area is for writing your thoughts and feelings about the information in this lesson. Please be honest with yourself. This exercise will help you understand and retain what you have read.

Thoughts and Feelings:

_____

_____

_____

_____

_____

_____

_____

_____

_____

_____

_____

**Lesson Verse: Proverbs 1:7**

"The fear of the Lord is the beginning of knowledge: but fools despise wisdom and instruction."

## Review

This is where the rubber meets the road. You must ask yourself how you will respond to the lesson.

Choose what you believe is the appropriate answer for you, and/or give an explanation of your answer in the space provided. Circle the answer where appropriate.

Explain how you feel we should act toward God?

_____

_____

How would you characterize the relationships you have had with other people in the past?

Strained
Comfortable
Conflicting
Respectful
Caring
Mutually beneficial

_____

_____

To what extent do you understand the role human nature plays in our actions and behaviors?

None
Some
Completely

_____

_____

Describe how you feel our human nature affects our relationship with God.

_____

_____

**TRUE or FALSE**

Truth ☉ Meter

Answer the following questions to the best of your ability. Some of these questions may be on the quiz at the end of the Pathway.

Please answer the following questions to the best of your ability. Write your answers in the spaces provided.

1. Individuals possess unique _____ that belong to them only.

2. It is differences that God uses as different colored threads to weave a beautiful _____ __ _____ through time.

3. Knowing that God has a definite purpose for each person reveals ___ ____ He has for His creation.

4. It is true that God created man for _____ and to glorify Him.

5. God exists in _____ past, present, and future.

6. We are responsible for the _____ we make.

7. Man is accountable both to God and to his _____ ___ for his choices.

8. Realizing that we are accountable to God produces a _____ ___ _____ for God and the things of God.

9. What a man believes in his heart to be true about God, will determine how he _____ ___ _____ with his fellow man as well as with God.

10. The only way a person can have a _____ with God is through His Son, Jesus Christ.

11. Becoming more like Christ is a process that takes place as you spend time with Him in _____ and _____ the Word of God.

12. A _____ life is a life that trusts, and rests, in God for all things.

106

Think about it!

This area is for writing your thoughts and feelings about the information in this lesson. Please be honest with yourself. This exercise will help you understand and retain what you have read.

Thoughts and Feelings:

_____
_____
_____
_____
_____
_____
_____
_____
_____
_____

**Lesson Verse: Romans 5:12**

"Wherefore, as by one man sin entered into the world, and death by sin; and so death passed upon all men, for that all have sinned."

## Review

This is where the rubber meets the road. You must ask yourself how you will respond to the lesson.

Choose what you believe is the appropriate answer for you, and/or give an explanation of your answer in the space provided. Circle the answer where appropriate.

Explain how Adam and Eve's decision to eat of the fruit affected everyone in the world.

_____

_____

_____

Describe a situation, that you know personally, where someone's actions affected someone else in an adverse way.

_____

_____

How did your knowledge of this situation make you feel?

_____

_____

Explain how addictions cause people to not contribute to society.

_____

_____

How would you describe your personal contributions to society?
  None
  Poor
  Average
  Excellent

_____

_____

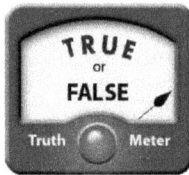

Answer the following questions to the best of your ability. Some of these questions may be on the quiz at the end of the Pathway.

Please answer the following questions to the best of your ability. Write your answers in the spaces provided.

1. To conclude that one's choices in life affect no one is simply a refusal to acknowledge ___ _____.

2. Other than the _____ __ _____ itself, the Bible tells us because of the sin of one man all men are separated from God.

3. This responsibility to our fellow man does not just extend toward those people we may know, but __ _____.

4. When a person who has life-controlling habits and behaviors fails to contribute to the progress of the society in which he lives, he becomes _ _____ to that society. a

5. When a person is controlled by a habit or behavior, they think only about _____.

6. To not recognize the proper conduct toward other people is to fail in the _____ that God has ordained to exist.

7. By not recognizing our responsibility to other people for our conduct we are actually saying that we do not believe ___ __ ___ ____.

8. If our love for God is what it should be, we will not have any problems loving _____ _____.

**Think about it!**

This area is for writing your thoughts and feelings about the information in this lesson. Please be honest with yourself. This exercise will help you understand and retain what you have read.

Thoughts and Feelings:

_____

_____

_____

_____

_____

_____

_____

_____

_____

_____

**Lesson Verse: James 1:26**

"If any man among you seem to be religious, and bridleth not his tongue, but deceiveth his own heart, this man's religion is vain."

**Review**

Choose what you believe is the appropriate answer for you, and/or give an explanation of your answer in the space provided. Circle the answer where appropriate.

Describe some habits that you have now that you did not have before your addiction.

_____

_____

What do you feel are some good habits that you possess?

_____

_____

What is your personal definition of discipline?

_____

_____

Other than addiction behavior, what are some things to which you are much attached?

_____

_____

How does acting upon your attachment to these make you feel?
    Strong
    Fulfilled
    Happy
    Content
    Needed

_____

_____

Answer the following questions to the best of your ability. Some of these questions may be on the quiz at the end of the Pathway.

Please answer the following questions to the best of your ability. Write your answers in the spaces provided.

111

1. Habits are behaviors that take place _____ due to prolonged and duplicated activities and feelings.

2. There can be negative, _____ _____ as well as positive, constructive habits.

3. The process of real recovery takes place _____ _____, as the individual learns what behaviors are best for them.

4. These changes follow a _____ _____ with Jesus Christ.

5. The view that fleshly desires are simply manifestations of _____ is not a common view.

6. The discipline we need to have the right kind of thinking, actions, desires and beliefs comes from the _____ __ ___, as we allow it to control our lives.

7. _____ _____ is in constant battle with godly actions.

8. Our sinful nature, if not dealt with, may keep us _____ from God for eternity.

9. Personal discipline begins with having a relationship with the Creator that enables us to ___ _____ to our sinful nature.

# PATHWAY 5 - Review Test

1. Adam and Eve's decision to disobey God gave their children a ____ _____ to follow.

   _____

2. We must submit our will to God and allow Him to have control of our _____ and our _____.

   _____

3. It is true that God created man for _____ and to glorify Him.

   _____

4. Reverence and respect for God is called, "___ ____ __ ___."

   _____

5. When a person is controlled by a habit or behavior, they think only about _____.

   _____

6. Habits are behaviors that take place _____ due to prolonged and duplicated activities and feelings.

   _____

7. Personal discipline begins with having a relationship with the Creator that enables us to ___ _____ to our sinful nature.

   _____

# PATHWAY 6
# INSTRUCTION

## MILSTONE 32
## PURPOSE OF INSTRUCTION

**Think about it!**

This area is for writing your thoughts and feelings about the information in this lesson. Please be honest with yourself. This exercise will help you understand and retain what you have read.

Thoughts and Feelings:

_____

_____

_____

_____

_____

_____

**Lesson Verse: Proverbs 4:13**

"Take fast hold of instruction; let her not go: keep her; for she is thy life."

## Review

This is where the rubber meets the road. You must ask yourself how you will respond to the lesson.

Choose what you believe is the appropriate answer for you, and/or give an explanation of your answer in the space provided. Circle the answer where appropriate.

Name as many sources of instruction as you can.

_____

_____

_____

How obedient to authority were you as a child?
    Never
    Some
    Mostly
    Always

Describe a situation where you had to read the instructions in order to accomplish a task.

_____

_____

How well committed are you to personal relationships?
    Poor
    Some
    Average
    Good
    Very much

_____

_____

Explain what you believe to be the importance of information.

_____

_____

Explain the circumstances surrounding when you realized your need to seek help for your addiction.

_____

_____

115

TRUE
or
FALSE

Truth   Meter

Answer the following questions to the best of your ability. Some of these questions may be on the quiz at the end of the Pathway.

Please answer the following questions to the best of your ability. Write your answers in the spaces provided.

1. Because we are accountable for ____ _____, we need to understand where instruction comes from, why it is important, and how obedience affects our lives.

2. Satan is a master at _____.

3. Eventually the addict realizes their life is really out of control and everything they have worked to accomplish is __ _____ because of their addiction.

4. As the creature, we have a responsibility to be _____ __ ____ as the Creator.

5. The purpose of _____ is to gain the knowledge necessary to make right decisions.

6. The most important knowledge you can gain is the knowledge necessary to make a decision about _____ __ ____ _____.

7. It is the ___ of information that makes it _____.

8. Information is only _____ ____ that has no significance until it is organized into a meaningful structure.

9. When combined with _____, knowledge creates more actions that are pleasing to God.

116

**Think about it!**

This area is for writing your thoughts and feelings about the information in this lesson. Please be honest with yourself. This exercise will help you understand and retain what you have read.

Thoughts and Feelings:

_____

_____

_____

_____

_____

_____

_____

_____

_____

_____

**Lesson Verse: John 1:1-2**

"In the beginning was the Word, and the Word was with God, and the Word was God. The same was in the beginning with God."

## Review

This is where the rubber meets the road. You must ask yourself how you will respond to the lesson.

Choose what you believe is the appropriate answer for you, and/or give an explanation of your answer in the space provided. Circle the answer where appropriate.

What do you believe to be the importance of the "Ten Commandments," if any?

_____

_____

Why do you think the Bible is important to the subject of instruction?

_____

_____

Do you believe in God? Why or why not?

Yes

No

_____

_____

Why do you believe God placed man on the earth?

_____

_____

Explain in your own words what you believe our responsibility is to God.

_____

_____

TRUE
or
FALSE

Truth Meter

Answer the following questions to the best of your ability. Some of these questions may be on the quiz at the end of the Pathway.

Please answer the following questions to the best of your ability. Write your answers in the spaces provided.

1. At the time of Adam and Eve, God's instructions were given _____.

2. One of the first examples of the written Word is seen when God wrote the ___ _____ on the stone tablets and gave them to Moses.

3. In writing the Bible, God used over __ different writers spanning a period of ____ years, with all content and themes in agreement.

4. God reveals to us in His Word as much about _____ as he desired.

5. He has revealed humanity's ____, _____ and _____ as they pertain to our relationship with Him.

6. It is through a careful study of the Bible and time spent in prayer we find a _____ and _____ relationship with God's Son, Jesus Christ.

7. The Scripture is very clear that Jesus Christ was and is the eternal ____ __ ___.

**Think about it!**

This area is for writing your thoughts and feelings about the information in this lesson. Please be honest with yourself. This exercise will help you understand and retain what you have read.

Thoughts and Feelings:

_____

_____

_____

_____

_____

_____

_____

_____

_____

_____

_____

**Lesson Verse: 2Timothy 3:16**

"All scripture is given by inspiration of God, and is profitable for doctrine, for reproof, for correction, for instruction in righteousness:"

**Review**

This is where the rubber meets the road. You must ask yourself how you will respond to the lesson.

Choose what you believe is the appropriate answer for you, and/or give an explanation of your answer in the space provided. Circle the answer where appropriate.

How important do you believe the Bible is to our daily lives?
    None
    Some
    Very

_____

_____

How much of what the Bible teaches do you feel you already obey?
    None
    Some
    Much
    All

_____

_____

From where do you believe is the most important source of instruction on how to live?
    Parents
    Society
    Bible
    Government
    Experience

_____

_____

Do you believe God has the power to completely deliver you from your addiction?
    Yes
    No

```
 ┌─────────────┐
 │  T R U E    │
 │    or       │
 │  FALSE      │
 │             │
 │ Truth ● Meter│
 └─────────────┘
```

Answer the following questions to the best of your ability. Some of these questions may be on the quiz at the end of the Pathway.

Please answer the following questions to the best of your ability. Write your answers in the spaces provided.

1. There are no _____ or _____ in the Bible.

2. The Word of God teaches us how to ____ ___ in return for how much He loves us.

3. We demonstrate our love for God by being _____ to his commandments.

4. God's written instructions are _____ and scientifically accurate.

5. His instructions are for not only how to live, but ___ __ ___ as well.

6. The reason we study and obey God's instructions is to please Him and open our life to ___ _____.

7. When a person is born into this world, they are not born with the _____ necessary to carry them through life.

8. The Scripture is where we find the _____ to life-controlling habits and behaviors.

9. God desires that we live our lives free from the _____ __ ___.

10. You must believe that God is who He says He is, and that He alone has the power to _____ you from the bondage of life-controlling habits.

122

**Think about it!**

This area is for writing your thoughts and feelings about the information in this lesson. Please be honest with yourself. This exercise will help you understand and retain what you have read.

Thoughts and Feelings:

_____

_____

_____

_____

_____

_____

_____

_____

_____

_____

**Lesson Verse: John 14:6**

"Jesus saith unto him, I am the way, the truth, and the life: no man cometh unto the Father, but by me."

**Review**

This is where the rubber meets the road. You must ask yourself how you will respond to the lesson.

Choose what you believe is the appropriate answer for you, and/or give an explanation of your answer in the space provided. Circle the answer where appropriate.

As a child, in what ways were you taught to obey?

_____

_____

_____

What dominant authorities were present in your life when you were a child?

_____

_____

What role models, beside parents, did you have growing up as a child?

_____

_____

What do you understand to be the role of government in our lives?

_____

_____

Describe some things in nature that you believe can give people instructions.

_____

_____

TRUE
or
FALSE

Truth     Meter

Answer the following questions to the best of your ability. Some of these questions may be on the quiz at the end of the Pathway.

Please answer the following questions to the best of your ability. Write your answers in the spaces provided.

1. God desires that men reach their full _____.

2. The only thing necessary for us to receive the ___ _____ from the Creator is to believe what He says concerning his Son, Jesus Christ, and follow the instructions in the Bible He has given to us concerning life.

3. The reason why it is God's instructions we must follow is because He is the one who _____ __.

4. As a child, we are taught to be obedient to our parents so we can learn to be obedient to God as __ _____.

5. It is because of this _____ we are able to receive the blessings of the Lord.

6. _____ ____ is the source of all instruction; however, God uses various means by which to instruct us.

7. The strong _____ ____ makes a strong Church and Nation.

8. God chooses to instruct those who are _____ by His Spirit.

9. Freedom to make choices is one _____ that separates us from the animals God created.

10. Humans possess a _____ _____ concerning harmful circumstances.

11. The reason God gives us instruction is so we may be able to enjoy the _____ that _____ to His instruction gives.

**Think about it!**

This area is for writing your thoughts and feelings about the information in this lesson. Please be honest with yourself. This exercise will help you understand and retain what you have read.

Thoughts and Feelings:

_____

_____

_____

_____

_____

_____

_____

_____

_____

_____

_____

**Lesson Verse: Psalm 25:21**

**"Let integrity and uprightness preserve me; for I wait on thee."**

## Review

This is where the rubber meets the road. You must ask yourself how you will respond to the lesson.

Choose what you believe is the appropriate answer for you, and/or give an explanation of your answer in the space provided. Circle the answer where appropriate.

How strong do you feel is your personal sense of self-preservation?
None
Some
Significant
Extremely high

_____

_____

What is your highest level of education?
High School or below
Some college
Associate degree
Undergraduate degree
Graduate degree (Master)
Advanced (Doctoral)

What physical side effects have you experienced as a result of your addiction?

_____

_____

What do you believe to be your personality type?
Protective
Creative
Intellectual
Visionary

_____

_____

What emotional type would you characterize yourself to be?

      Introverted (recluse, doesn't like crowds, quiet, etc.)

      Extroverted (outgoing, loves crowds, socially active, etc.)

_____

_____

How would you rate your physical condition?

      Poor

      Average

      Healthy

_____

_____

**TRUE** or **FALSE**
Truth Meter

Answer the following questions to the best of your ability. Some of these questions may be on the quiz at the end of the Pathway.

Please answer the following questions to the best of your ability. Write your answers in the spaces provided.

1. _____ is one of the strongest instincts present in human nature.

2. Disruption of proper thinking processes brought on by addiction, results in abnormal thinking or _____ _____.

3. The lack of education may predispose some individuals to _____ _____, but clearly, it is still a choice the individual makes.

4. While certain personalities are more susceptible to a continuation of harmful activities than others are, we must not forget that man has a ____ to _____.

5. Instruction is only as effective as the participant is able to _____ and understand the information.

6. Overcoming _____ _____ require a healthy diet, exercise, clean living, and obedience to instruction in righteousness.

# PATHWAY 6 - Review Test

1. Satan is a master at _____.

_____

2. The purpose of _____ is to gain the knowledge necessary to make right decisions.

_____

3. As you yield to God, He will _____ you to become more and more like His Son, Jesus Christ.

_____

4. At the time of Adam and Eve, God's instructions were given _____.

_____

5. He has revealed humanity's ____, _____ and _____ as they pertain to our relationship with Him.

_____

6. There are no _____ or _____ in the Bible.

_____

7. The reason we study and obey God's instructions is to please Him and open our life to ___ _____.

_____

8. The Scripture is where we find the _____ to life-controlling habits and behaviors.

_____

9. _____ is the source of all instruction; however, God uses various means by which to instruct us.

_____

# PATHWAY 7
# OBEDIENCE

## MILSTONE 37
## OBEDIENCE=FREEDOM

**Think about it!**

This area is for writing your thoughts and feelings about the information in this lesson. Please be honest with yourself. This exercise will help you understand and retain what you have read.

Thoughts and Feelings:

_____

_____

_____

_____

_____

_____

**Lesson Verse: Romans 6:16**

"Know ye not, that to whom ye yield yourselves servants to obey, his servants ye are to whom ye obey; whether of sin unto death, or of obedience unto righteousness?"

**Review**

This is where the rubber meets the road. You must ask yourself how you will respond to the lesson.

Choose what you believe is the appropriate answer for you, and/or give an explanation of your answer in the space provided. Circle the answer where appropriate.

Describe a situation where you took the lead and others followed.

_____

_____

Explain what it means to you to be held accountable for your actions.

_____

_____

In what ways have you searched for peace in your life?

_____

_____

How important to you is having freedom in our country to move around and pursue your dreams?

None

Some

Very

Extremely

_____

_____

TRUE
or
FALSE

Truth    Meter

Answer the following questions to the best of your ability. Some of these questions may be on the quiz at the end of the Pathway.

Please answer the following questions to the best of your ability. Write your answers in the spaces provided.

1. Without _____, there cannot be freedom.

2. Obedience is the essential part of _____.

3. We are to obey every law of man that does not _____ with the laws of God.

4. The more we follow the laws of the land, the more _____ we have to conduct our affairs with other men and live productive lives for the benefit of our society.

5. When we are obedient to ___, there is freedom.

6. The closer we follow God, the more He _____ our lives in the right paths.

7. Only through obedience to God's instructions can we find _____ in life and with God.

132

Think about it!

This area is for writing your thoughts and feelings about the information in this lesson. Please be honest with yourself. This exercise will help you understand and retain what you have read.

Thoughts and Feelings:

_____

_____

_____

_____

_____

_____

_____

_____

_____

_____

_____

**Lesson Verse: Galatians 5:13**

"For, brethren, ye have been called unto liberty; only use not liberty for an occasion to the flesh, but by love serve one another."

## Review

133

This is where the rubber meets the road. You must ask yourself how you will respond to the lesson.

Choose what you believe is the appropriate answer for you, and/or give an explanation of your answer in the space provided. Circle the answer where appropriate.

Have you ever had your personal right violated? Explain.

Yes

No

_____

_____

Explain the difference between a right and a privilege.

_____

_____

In what ways have members of your family paid for your addiction problems?

_____

_____

In what ways do you feel you can yield your will to God?

_____

_____

What do you think would be some positive results of yielding your will to God?

_____

_____

**TRUE** or **FALSE**

Truth Meter

Answer the following questions to the best of your ability. Some of these questions may be on the quiz at the end of the Pathway.

Please answer the following questions to the best of your ability. Write your answers in the spaces provided.

1. There is an inner part of man that God created, which cannot live under the ____ __ _____ and servitude.

2. _____ is the prize for all sane men, regardless of the cost.

3. Because our society has been blessed by God beyond our Founding Fathers' wildest imaginations, people have mistaken these blessings for _____.

4. Because God created man in His image, man has the right to carry out the purpose for having been created, without the hindrances, constraints and _____ of other men.

5. There must be an _____ between all men to allow the other to freely carry out his or her purpose for which they were created.

6. God-given responsibilities never _____, and therefore, God-given freedoms do not either.

7. A person's right to ____ means that every person has the same right to live.

8. When society has to pay for the consequences of addiction behavior, all people are affected in _____ ways.

9. We have the responsibility as Christians to yield our rights to God and allow Him to control the _____ as well as the results.

10. When we yield our rights to God, He frees us from the _____ of choice, leaving our _____ clear to serve Him and others with a pure heart.

**Think about it!**

This area is for writing your thoughts and feelings about the information in this lesson. Please be honest with yourself. This exercise will help you understand and retain what you have read.

Thoughts and Feelings:

_____

_____

_____

_____

_____

_____

_____

_____

_____

_____

_____

**Lesson Verse: Job 37:16**

"Dost thou know the balancings of the clouds, the wondrous works of him which is perfect in knowledge?"

## Review

This is where the rubber meets the road. You must ask yourself how you will respond to the lesson.

Choose what you believe is the appropriate answer for you, and/or give an explanation of your answer in the space provided. Circle the answer where appropriate.

Tell about a situation where you thought you knew the truth, but found out later that you did not, resulting in you being embarrassed.

_____

_____

_____

What are some ways that you feel God has protected you in the past?

_____

_____

How would you describe your personal level of humility?
Low
Average
High

_____

_____

What is your level of desire to be free from addictions?
None
Some
High

_____

_____

**TRUE or FALSE**
Truth — Meter

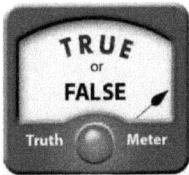

Answer the following questions to the best of your ability. Some of these questions may be on the quiz at the end of the Pathway.

Please answer the following questions to the best of your ability. Write your answers in the spaces provided.

1. Man has always believed he _____ _____ than God, especially when it comes to things that affect his personal life.

2. The only way in which we can know that God is working in our life is to have a personal _____ with Him.

3. To have the _____ of Christ requires that we know the Word of God.

4. God's _____ is infinite.

5. Our minds can only hold a certain amount of knowledge and _____.

6. While the capacity of the human brain is staggering, it is only a _____ or likeness of the infinite knowledge which God possess.

7. When we describe the knowledge of God, we use the term _____.

8. Knowing that we are important and _____ to God lets us know that it is the desire of God to take care of us.

9. When we surrender our will to make choices to God, we are showing our trust and _____ upon God.

10. Trusting in God for everything shows _____.

11. God's grace is sufficient for every situation and _____ in our life.

12. _____ is simply failing to maintain a daily relationship with Jesus Christ through Bible study and prayer.

138

**Think about it!**

This area is for writing your thoughts and feelings about the information in this lesson. Please be honest with yourself. This exercise will help you understand and retain what you have read.

Thoughts and Feelings:

_____

_____

_____

_____

_____

_____

_____

_____

_____

_____

**Lesson Verse: Acts 17:25**

"Neither is worshipped with men's hands, as though he needed any thing, seeing he giveth to all life, and breath, and all things;"

## Review

This is where the rubber meets the road. You must ask yourself how you will respond to the lesson.

Choose what you believe is the appropriate answer for you, and/or give an explanation of your answer in the space provided. Circle the answer where appropriate.

Have you ever attended an AA meeting?
Yes
No

What do you feel attending these meetings did for you?

_____

_____

Have you ever attended a rehab program in the past?
Yes
No

_____

_____

If yes, do you feel the rehab program you attended provided the help you needed?
Yes
No

_____

_____

If no, do you believe attending a rehab would have been helpful to you?
Yes
No

_____

_____

Answer the following questions to the best of your ability. Some of these questions may be on the quiz at the end of the Pathway.

Please answer the following questions to the best of your ability. Write your answers in the spaces provided.

1. Dependency on a 12-step program, or any program other than a Biblical one, is nothing more than just another _____.

2. When a program or curriculum places the emphasis on a list of _____ instead of on the Lord Jesus Christ and God's Word, they have lost the real _____ to free a man from life-controlling habits.

3. We should not _____ anything that helps people better themselves.

4. In helping a person prepare for _____, we help them live free from life-controlling habits now.

5. God has given us the _____ to every problem and question we face in life.

6. Victory over addictions is obtained through the power of the gospel of Jesus Christ manifested in a _____ ____.

7. When people believe they can cure addiction behaviors through man-made and man-centered _____, they miss the mark completely.

8. God desires that you live free from _____ _____, even when you are to blame.

9. Any program that does not acknowledge that God is the _____ for the cure to addictions, will fail miserably in giving their clients the truth.

10. The difference in secular and Biblical based programs is the _____ by which recovery is taught to the addict.

**Think about it!**

141

This area is for writing your thoughts and feelings about the information in this lesson. Please be honest with yourself. This exercise will help you understand and retain what you have read.

Thoughts and Feelings:

_____

_____

_____

_____

_____

_____

_____

_____

_____

_____

_____

**Lesson Verse: Romans 6:16**

Know ye not, that to whom ye yield yourselves servants to obey, his servants ye are to whom ye obey; whether of sin unto death, or of obedience unto righteousness?

**Review**

This is where the rubber meets the road. You must ask yourself how you will respond to the lesson.

Choose what you believe is the appropriate answer for you, and/or give an explanation of your answer in the space provided. Circle the answer where appropriate.

142

Briefly explain the circumstances of how and when you addiction behaviors began.

_____

_____

_____

What role, if any, did peer pressure have in the early stages of your addiction behaviors?

    None

    Some

    Much

_____

_____

What, if anything, could you have done differently to prevent the start of your addiction behaviors?

_____

_____

Did you feel that you were in control of your addiction, in the early stages?

    Yes

    No

_____

_____

What does it mean to you for God to be in control of your life?

_____

_____

Answer the following questions to the best of your ability. Some of these questions may be on the quiz at the end of the Pathway.

Please answer the following questions to the best of your ability. Write your answers in the spaces provided.

143

1. _____ is more commonly the strongest reason why people choose to participate in an illicit behavior.

2. Peer pressure is one of the strongest influences in the life of _____ as well.

3. The life that God desires that we live takes daily _____ and "dying" to self.

4. If we are truly going to "bear our cross," we must first learn how to ___ __ ____.

5. To bear our cross or die to self means that we place our body, along with its desires, under _____.

6. When we are faithful in having our daily time with the Lord in this way, God changes our desires from ones that love worldly _____ into desires that want to please Jesus Christ.

7. As we obediently surrender to what we learn in the Word of God, God gives us the _____ we need to face the temptations and trials of life.

8. As we get stronger in our Christian life, we lose the wrong desires that once ruled our _____ and actions.

144

**Think about it!**

This area is for writing your thoughts and feelings about the information in this lesson. Please be honest with yourself. This exercise will help you understand and retain what you have read.

Thoughts and Feelings:

_____

_____

_____

_____

_____

_____

_____

_____

_____

_____

**Lesson Verse: Romans 5:21**

"That as sin hath reigned unto death, even so might grace reign through righteousness unto eternal life by Jesus Christ our Lord."

## Review

This is where the rubber meets the road. You must ask yourself how you will respond to the lesson.

Choose what you believe is the appropriate answer for you, and/or give an explanation of your answer in the space provided. Circle the answer where appropriate.

How would you characterize your relationship with your parents or guardians?
Passive
Loving
Disciplined
Non-existent

_____

_____

How many siblings, if any, do you have? Explain where you fit into the age range.

_____

_____

How would you characterize your relationship with your siblings?
Non-existent
Amicable
Passive
Close

_____

_____

Are there any consequences for your addiction behaviors for which you feel you will still have to pay? If so, what are they?
Yes
No

_____

_____

What physical or emotional consequences have you already gone through, if any?

_____

_____

TRUE
or
FALSE

Truth    Meter

Answer the following questions to the best of your ability. Some of these questions may be on the quiz at the end of the Pathway.

146

Please answer the following questions to the best of your ability. Write your answers in the spaces provided.

1. When a Believer in Christ commits sins of addiction, or any sin for that matter, _____ with God is broken because of this disobedience.

2. When we are born again into the family of God, we are given a new _____.

3. Not only are we given a new nature, but we are also pardoned from the _____ of sin, which is death.

4. Christ paid for this pardon with ___ _____ on the cross of Calvary.

5. When a member of God's family disobeys God, the fellowship with God is broken and they are _____ by God, but they remain in His family.

6. God desires that we accept His free gift of _____.

7. "For the wages of sin is death; but the gift of God is _____ _____through Jesus Christ our Lord."

8. The law of sowing and _____ applies to Believers and non-Believers alike.

9. Becoming a Christian does not remove the responsibility of doing right or the _____ of doing wrong.

# PATHWAY 7 - Review Test

1. Without _____, there cannot be freedom.

_____

2. Because our society has been blessed by God beyond our Founding Fathers' wildest imaginations, people have mistaken these blessings for _____.

_____

3. God-given responsibilities never _____, and therefore, God-given freedoms do not either.

_____

4. The only way in which we can know that God is working in our life is to have a personal _____ with Him.

_____

5. Trusting in God for everything shows _____.

_____

6. _____ is simply failing to maintain a daily relationship with Jesus Christ through Bible study and prayer.

_____

7. Dependency on a 12-step program, or any program other than a Biblical one, is nothing more than just another _____.

_____

8. In helping a person prepare for _____, we help them live free from life-controlling habits now.

_____

9. If we are truly going to "bear our cross," we must first learn how to ___ __ ____.

_____

# PATHWAY 8
# ADDICTION CYCLES

## MILSTONE 43
## DENIAL OF ADDICTION

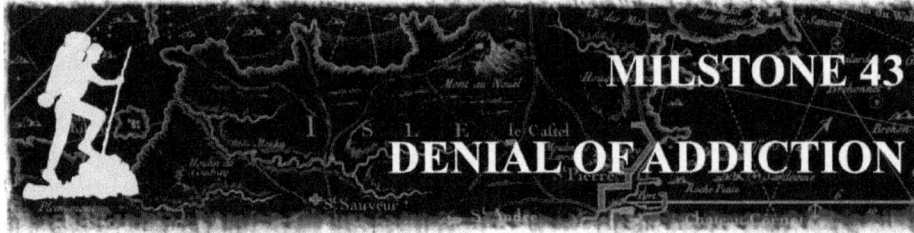

**Think about it!**

This area is for writing your thoughts and feelings about the information in this lesson. Please be honest with yourself. This exercise will help you understand and retain what you have read.

Thoughts and Feelings:

_____

_____

_____

_____

_____

_____

Lesson Verse: 1Thessalonians 5:21-22

"Prove all things; hold fast that which is good. Abstain from all appearance of evil."

## Review

This is where the rubber meets the road. You must ask yourself how you will respond to the lesson.

Choose what you believe is the appropriate answer for you, and/or give an explanation of your answer in the space provided. Circle the answer where appropriate.

Do you consider yourself to be a functioning addict, or a non-functioning addict? Why?

Functioning

Non-functioning

_____

_____

Did social acceptance play a part in the creation of your addiction behaviors?

Yes

No

_____

_____

Did escape from pressures of daily life play a role in the beginning of your addiction behaviors?

Yes

No

_____

_____

At this point in your addiction, have you faced the denial stage?

Yes

No

How willing are you to admit that your addiction problems begin and end with you?

Not

Maybe

Yes

_____

_____

**TRUE**
or
**FALSE**

Truth    Meter

Answer the following questions to the best of your ability. Some of these questions may be on the quiz at the end of the Pathway.

Please answer the following questions to the best of your ability. Write your answers in the spaces provided.

1. There is a stage in the addiction cycle where the addict does not _____ they are an addict.

2. Very few people actually like the _____ of alcohol on their first drink.

3. The most common reason for drinking is _____ acceptance.

4. The stage of "_____ _____," is a precursor to the "non-functioning" addict.

5. There is an affection with addictions that is stronger, in most cases, than the natural _____ one may have with other people.

6. Just as with human relationships, the addict will spend an enormous amount of ____ with their addiction.

7. The use of alcohol as a beverage can, not only result in an addiction in the life of a Christian, but it can also be an _____ for a weaker Christian.

**Think about it!**

This area is for writing your thoughts and feelings about the information in this lesson. Please be honest with yourself. This exercise will help you understand and retain what you have read.

151

Thoughts and Feelings:

_____

_____

_____

_____

_____

_____

_____

_____

_____

_____

_____

**Lesson Verse: Romans 12:2**

"And be not conformed to this world: but be ye transformed by the renewing of your mind, that ye may prove what is that good, and acceptable, and perfect, will of God."

## Review

This is where the rubber meets the road. You must ask yourself how you will respond to the lesson.

Choose what you believe is the appropriate answer for you, and/or give an explanation of your answer in the space provided. Circle the answer where appropriate.

That you are aware of, who knew about the onset of your addiction?

None

Only family members

Only coworkers

Both family and coworkers

Of the people that knew about the beginning of your addictions problems, did any of them try and find help for you? If so, who?

Yes

No

_____

_____

Are you aware of a church in your area that provides a weekly support meeting for addicts? If so, what is the name of the church?

Yes

No

_____

How important do you feel attending church is to your recovery process?

None

Little

Some

Very

At this point, how much control do you feel your addiction has over your actions and behaviors?

None

Slight

Moderate
Heavy
Complete

_____

_____

TRUE
or
FALSE

Truth    Meter

Answer the following questions to the best of your ability. Some of these questions may be on the quiz at the end of the Pathway.

Please answer the following questions to the best of your ability. Write your answers in the spaces provided.

1.  Life-controlling habits are _____ and subtle in their control over the addict.

2.  When the addiction matures, which happens extremely fast with some behaviors, the addict loses a significant amount of _____ over their personal actions.

3.  The body's desire for the chemical of choice, whether alcohol or other drug, is the result of a loss of control, but not a complete _____ of control.

4.  The distinction that needs to be made is that people who are in the _____ __ ___ have the same ability to allow addictions in their life as non-Believers have.

5.  The person who does not have the Holy Spirit indwelling them does not have the ___ _____ and, therefore, have only the sinful, fallen nature that guides their actions and behaviors.

6.  People who can perform their responsibilities in a reasonable manner are who we call _____ addicts.

7.  There are life-controlling behaviors that result from influences other than _____ influences.

8.  There are also psychological influences that result in _____ _____ and habits.

154

**Think about it!**

This area is for writing your thoughts and feelings about the information in this lesson. Please be honest with yourself. This exercise will help you understand and retain what you have read.

Thoughts and Feelings:

_____

_____

_____

_____

_____

_____

_____

_____

_____

_____

**Lesson Verse: Jeremiah 31:3**

"The LORD hath appeared of old unto me, saying, Yea, I have loved thee with an everlasting love: therefore with lovingkindness have I drawn thee."

## Review

This is where the rubber meets the road. You must ask yourself how you will respond to the lesson.

Choose what you believe is the appropriate answer for you, and/or give an explanation of your answer in the space provided. Circle the answer where appropriate.

How has your addiction behaviors affected your job performance?
    None
    Some
    Greatly

_____

_____

How much money would you estimate that you have spent on your addiction since the beginning?
    No idea
    Hundreds
    Thousands
    Over ten thousand
    Over fifty Thousand
    Over one hundred Thousand

_____

_____

Briefly describe any circumstances, of which you are personally aware, where someone died as a direct result of their addiction.

_____

_____

What, if any, psychological effect has your addiction had on you personally?

_____

_____

Are you willing to allow God to have control over your actions and behaviors?

Yes

No

_____

_____

Answer the following questions to the best of your ability. Some of these questions may be on the quiz at the end of the Pathway.

Please answer the following questions to the best of your ability. Write your answers in the spaces provided.

1.  Many times the addict will blame _____ that take place in their life for their addiction.

2.  The addict must face the fact that they are both the _____ of the addiction and the _____ of the solution to the addiction.

3.  Physical and psychological influences are limited in their effect based upon your level of _____ of them in your life.

4.  We all have the opportunity to allow God the freedom to _____ our lives.

5.  We have the ability to choose the direction of our lives based upon our will as a free_____ _____.

6.  The choices we make in life are a direct reflection of what we _____ _____ ___ and who we believe He is.

7.  If we believe that God is a holy and _____ God who will call us to give an accounting of our life, to the best of our ability, we will live a life that is pleasing to Him.

8. If we believe that God does not exist and that we will not give an account for our actions, we will live according to the _____ of the flesh and the dictates of our sinful nature.

9. Because God is a good God and He loves us with an infinite love, He not only gives us the ability to understand the differences in the consequences of our actions, but He gives us the ability to choose the _____ and _____ of our life.

10. You have the freedom of choice that should be exercised for things that are _____ and _____, rather than for things that are in conflict with God.

158

**Think about it!**

This area is for writing your thoughts and feelings about the information in this lesson. Please be honest with yourself. This exercise will help you understand and retain what you have read.

Thoughts and Feelings:

_____

_____

_____

_____

_____

_____

_____

_____

_____

_____

**Lesson Verse: Mark 12:30**

"And thou shalt love the Lord thy God with all thy heart, and with all thy soul, and with all thy mind, and with all thy strength: this is the first commandment."

## Review

This is where the rubber meets the road. You must ask yourself how you will respond to the lesson.

Choose what you believe is the appropriate answer for you, and/or give an explanation of your answer in the space provided. Circle the answer where appropriate.

Explain what it means to you to say that your addiction is a relationship you have.

_____

_____

_____

At what stage in the addiction do you feel you are?
Denial
Bargaining
Anger
Grief/Depression
Acceptance

_____

_____

Describe a situation where you employed bargaining to continue your addiction activities.

_____

_____

Has there ever been a time in which you bargained with God? Explain.
Yes
No

_____

_____

Are there actions and behaviors for which you need forgiveness from another person?
Yes
No

Answer the following questions to the best of your ability. Some of these questions may be on the quiz at the end of the Pathway.

160

Please answer the following questions to the best of your ability. Write your answers in the spaces provided.

1. Those who commit themselves to a rehab or recovery program are faced with the same _____ battle as one who has lost a loved one might face.

2. When a relationship is severed, there is a natural process of _____ that takes place.

3. _____ is a self-preservation mechanism triggered in an attempt to resist or avoid the truth.

4. _____ is typically a reaction by a person who is at a stage where they do not realize the reality of their condition.

5. Any level of bargaining results in the _____ of any positive movement toward recovery.

6. God's laws do not change and they are _____; we do not bargain with God.

7. God still demands and deserves ____ _____ in the lives of His creation.

8. Anger is one of the basic of all human _____.

9. It is possible to use the emotion of anger to change a _____ that needs correcting.

10. A person should never hold on to the emotion of anger because it can very quickly turn into _____.

11. _____ is an emotion that most people only associate with the loss of a loved one or close friend.

12. The grieving process is important to the progression toward the _____ stage.

13. _____ is necessary to understand God's truth about recovery.

162

**Think about it!**

This area is for writing your thoughts and feelings about the information in this lesson. Please be honest with yourself. This exercise will help you understand and retain what you have read.

Thoughts and Feelings:

_____
_____
_____
_____
_____
_____
_____
_____
_____
_____
_____

**Lesson Verse: Proverbs 9:10**

**"The fear of the LORD *is* the beginning of wisdom: and the knowledge of the holy *is* understanding."**

## Review

Choose what you believe is the appropriate answer for you, and/or give an explanation of your answer in the space provided. Circle the answer where appropriate.

163

Describe a situation where you felt one of the three emotions of guilt, fear or shame, as a direct result of your addiction.

_____

_____

_____

How do you feel society views addicts and addictions in general?

_____

_____

What role, if any, did any of the three emotions of guilt, fear or shame, play in the start of your addiction behaviors?

None

Some

Much

_____

_____

Does the fear of relapse keep you from the belief that you can be totally free from addictions?

Yes

No

_____

_____

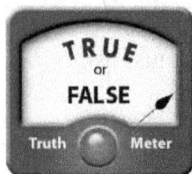

Answer the following questions to the best of your ability. Some of these questions may be on the quiz at the end of the Pathway.

Please answer the following questions to the best of your ability. Write your answers in the spaces provided.

164

1. The primary reason the addict feels guilt is because they know that their behavior is not _____ in society.

2. Anyone who allows themselves to participate in addiction-generating activities also has the same _____ for becoming an addict as well.

3. In the addict's mind, the only way to remove this feeling of guilt is to hide it under another _____ of addiction.

4. Guilt can actually be a good _____ in helping you through the recovery process.

5. Fear is a very powerful emotion. It causes or can even force us to _____ our position.

6. Fear of the _____ is usually the most prevailing fear in all humans.

7. This program is the right beginning to dispel further fears in your life, but the ultimate fear is the ____ __ ___.

8. When we have the right fear of God, it removes all other fears in our life because we know that God is _____ than all others.

9. Shame is one of those emotions that can drastically effect a person's ability to recognize their personal _____ to God.

10. Excessive shame can mask the real _____ of a person to such a degree that they lose their belief that they have value as a person.

11. By placing your _____ ___ _____ in Jesus Christ as your Saviour, God gives you a new nature that hears when He speaks to you.

**Think about it!**

This area is for writing your thoughts and feelings about the information in this lesson. Please be honest with yourself. This exercise will help you understand and retain what you have read.

Thoughts and Feelings:

_____

_____

_____

_____

_____

_____

_____

_____

_____

_____

**Lesson Verse: Acts 3:19**

"Repent ye therefore, and be converted, that your sins may be blotted out, when the times of refreshing shall come from the presence of the Lord;"

## Review

This is where the rubber meets the road. You must ask yourself how you will respond to the lesson.

Choose what you believe is the appropriate answer for you, and/or give an explanation of your answer in the space provided. Circle the answer where appropriate.

166

Do you consider yourself to be a "recovering" addict? Why?

Yes

No

_____

_____

_____

Do you now, or have you in the past, felt that you have the strength to heal yourself from your addiction problems?

Yes

Now

_____

_____

Do you believe that if you continue down the path of addiction behaviors, you will ultimately perish as a result?

Yes

No

_____

_____

**TRUE** or **FALSE**

Truth Meter

Answer the following questions to the best of your ability. Some of these questions may be on the quiz at the end of the Pathway.

Please answer the following questions to the best of your ability. Write your answers in the spaces provided.

1. For you to love God enough to change your _____, you must first see the love of God.

2. The first place you will see the love of Christ manifested is in the _____ of those people that desire to help you.

3. The ____ __ _____ should be a natural part of any person's life that desires to help other people overcome life-controlling habits.

4. When we have a close relationship with the Lord, He reminds us of our own _____ and need for humility.

5. Recovery is not the goal. Recovery is the _____ of non-addiction behavior.

6. Recovery is the by-product of something much more _____ in a person's life. Recovery is the result of a life _____ to God.

7. When a person yields their will to the will of God, they place themselves in the wonderful position of _____ _____ from the Creator.

8. When a person is _____, they only attain as much recovery as they can muster in and of themselves.

9. Transformation is completely of ____.

10. Before you can experience freedom from life-controlling habits through the process of transformation and sanctification, you must first have a _____ to receive help.

11. Many addicts want a _____ life, but are not willing to give up the addiction to have it.

12. _____ is simply acknowledging who God is and that you are a sinner that needs Jesus Christ as your Saviour.

168

**Think about it!**

This area is for writing your thoughts and feelings about the information in this lesson. Please be honest with yourself. This exercise will help you understand and retain what you have read.

Thoughts and Feelings:

_____

_____

_____

_____

_____

_____

_____

_____

_____

**Lesson Verse: Philippians 3:13-14**

Brethren, I count not myself to have apprehended: but this one thing I do, forgetting those things which are behind, and reaching forth unto those things which are before, I press toward the mark for the prize of the high calling of God in Christ Jesus.

## Review

This is where the rubber meets the road. You must ask yourself how you will respond to the lesson.

Choose what you believe is the appropriate answer for you, and/or give an explanation of your answer in the space provided. Circle the answer where appropriate.

What traits in your life do you recognize are a direct result of addiction activities?

_____

_____

How many separate types of addictions do you believe you have? Explain

_____

_____

What level of stress overall has your addiction caused in your life?

None

Minimal

Some

Much

Extreme

_____

_____

Do you find yourself withdrawing from certain people or circumstances so as to not be discovered to be an addict? Explain why or why not.

Yes

No

_____

_____

How often have you needed to borrow money to continue your addiction behaviors?

Never

Seldom

Occasionally

Often

Explain a time when you had to borrow money to continue your addiction activities.

_____

_____

Do you recognize the need to begin helping others as a part of your own recovery process?

    Yes

    No

Describe in what ways you can help others become free from their own addiction problems.

_____

_____

Describe some of the behaviors given in the text that reflect your own behaviors.

_____

_____

**TRUE** or **FALSE**

Truth   Meter

Answer the following questions to the best of your ability. Some of these questions may be on the quiz at the end of the Pathway.

Please answer the following questions to the best of your ability. Write your answers in the spaces provided.

1. One of the important factors of breaking the addiction cycle is to recognize the _____ and behaviors that prevail in your life as an addict.

2. Many times a person who is struggling to keep their addiction hid will have a hard time keeping their _____ in check.

3. The last thing the addict wants to do is place themselves unnecessarily in a position of _____ with others.

4. Addiction to drugs and gambling can be the most _____ habits to maintain.

5. The Bible says, "The wages of sin is _____."

6. One of the more noticeable changes in the life of the addict is the type of _____ with which the addict is associated.

7. It is accurate to say that we _____ with those with whom we associate.

8. We identify with a certain group of people by the _____ __ ____.

9. Damage caused by a long-term cycle of drug and alcohol use results in the addict developing a strong sense of _____.

10. Most people can tell if someone else is genuinely _____ about them.

# PATHWAY 8 - Review Test

1.  The most common reason for drinking is _____ acceptance.

    _____

2.  Life-controlling habits are _____ and subtle in their control over the addict.

    _____

3.  Many times the addict will blame _____ that take place in their life for their addiction.

    _____

4.  The choices we make in life are a direct reflection of what we _____ _____ ___ and who we believe He is.

    _____

5.  _____ is a self-preservation mechanism triggered in an attempt to resist or avoid the truth.

    _____

6.  God's laws do not change and they are _____; we do not bargain with God.

    _____

7.  _____ is necessary to understand God's truth about recovery.

    _____

8.  Fear of the _____ is usually the most prevailing fear in all humans.

    _____

9.  Recovery is not the goal. Recovery is the _____ of non-addiction behavior.

    _____

10. Transformation is completely of ___.

    _____

## MILSTONE 50
## PHYSICAL EFFECTS

**Think about it!**

This area is for writing your thoughts and feelings about the information in this lesson. Please be honest with yourself. This exercise will help you understand and retain what you have read.

Thoughts and Feelings:

_____

_____

_____

_____

_____

_____

**Lesson Verse: Mark 8:36-37**

"For what shall it profit a man if he shall gain the whole world, and lose his own soul? Or what shall a man give in exchange for his soul?"

## Review

174

This is where the rubber meets the road. You must ask yourself how you will respond to the lesson.

Choose what you believe is the appropriate answer for you, and/or give an explanation of your answer in the space provided. Circle the answer where appropriate.

In what ways has your addiction affected your physical body?

_____

_____

Do you believe the emotional and mental effect your addiction has had on you is stronger than the physical effect? Explain.

Yes

No

_____

_____

How would knowing the future affect your decisions about your addiction?

_____

_____

Do you feel your addiction has diminished in any way your ability to reason and think? If so, in what ways?

Yes

No

_____

_____

How successful have you been in hiding your addiction behaviors?

None

Some

Very

_____

_____

Do you believe "False Logic" has affected you personally? If yes, in what way?

Yes

No

_____

_____

**TRUE**
or
**FALSE**

Truth    Meter

Answer the following questions to the best of your ability. Some of these questions may be on the quiz at the end of the Pathway.

Please answer the following questions to the best of your ability. Write your answers in the spaces provided.

1. The _____ effects of addictions are different for each person.

2. The mental and _____ effects addictions have on individuals are much more devastating because they last much longer than do the physical effects.

3. Satan deceived Eve into thinking she could satisfy her flesh, ignore the command of God, and not suffer the _____ of that decision.

4. The most devastating effect addiction has on the individual is not the physical death; it is the _____ death of separation from God.

5. There is no _____ available when a person dies without knowing Jesus Christ as their personal Saviour.

6. When a person dies without knowing Jesus Christ, the resulting separation from God is _____.

7. Satan's number one lie is that there is _____ to make things right with God.

8. There is no time other than the _____ to make things right with God.

9. It is in knowing God, and through His power alone, that cures the addict from the _____ of addiction.

10. There is a sense of _____ or shame that a person who is addicted to voyeurism or gambling carries with them.

11. The most common side effect of alcohol abuse is _____ of the liver.

12. God warns us in His Word against allowing our behaviors to become "_____ _____"‖ to the weaker Christian.

13. We must decide that our conduct is going to be _____, not just acceptable to others.

**Think about it!**

This area is for writing your thoughts and feelings about the information in this lesson. Please be honest with yourself. This exercise will help you understand and retain what you have read.

Thoughts and Feelings:

_____

_____

_____

_____

_____

_____

_____

_____

_____

_____

**Lesson Verse: Philippians 4:9**

"Those things, which ye have both learned, and received, and heard, and seen in me, do: and the God of peace shall be with you."

## Review

Choose what you believe is the appropriate answer for you, and/or give an explanation of your answer in the space provided. Circle the answer where appropriate.

What kind of habits have formed in your life as a direct result of addiction behaviors?

_____

_____

_____

What circumstances or individuals in your past were instrumental in your starting behaviors that resulted in addiction?

_____

_____

Do you believe that addictions are illnesses? Explain.

Yes

No

_____

_____

At what age do you believe you began to understand right from wrong behaviors?

Before 5 years of age

Before 7 years of age

Between 7 and 10 years of age

After 10 years of age

_____

_____

At what age did you become responsible for supporting yourself?

Before 15 years of age

Between 15 and 18 years of age

Between 18 and 25 years of age

After 25 years of age

_____

_____

TRUE
or
FALSE
Truth  Meter

Answer the following questions to the best of your ability.
Some of these questions may be on the quiz at the end of the
Pathway.

Please answer the following questions to the best of your ability. Write your answers in the
spaces provided.

1. We know that addictions are habits because they are _____ behaviors.

2. We learn the majority of our behaviors during our _____ years.

3. The reason we act out what we see and repeat what we hear is that they are repeated
   often enough that we learn to _____ them.

4. When a person reaches a certain age, they have the ability to _____ whether their
   behaviors are good or bad.

5. The age of _____ is the age when a person knows their actions have
   consequences, and they know the difference between right and wrong behaviors.

6. Man learns from his mistakes, and when he is not held accountable for his mistakes,
   he either learns nothing at all, or learns to _____ his actions.

7. When those in authority consider certain behaviors as _____, man learns to
   place the blame for his actions onto someone or something other than himself.

8. Man has learned that if everyone could just ignore the _____ of their actions,
   no one can be held accountable for the actions that destroy.

9. Addictions are not _____.

10. Habits are formed when a person repeatedly performs any behavior, whether good or
    bad (positive or negative), over a _____ _____.

180

**Think about it!**

This area is for writing your thoughts and feelings about the information in this lesson. Please be honest with yourself. This exercise will help you understand and retain what you have read.

Thoughts and Feelings:

_____
_____
_____
_____
_____
_____
_____
_____
_____
_____

**Lesson Verse: Galatians 6:7-8**

"Be not deceived; God is not mocked: for whatsoever a man soweth, that shall he also reap. For he that soweth to his flesh shall of the flesh reap corruption; but he that soweth to the Spirit shall of the Spirit reap life everlasting."

**Review**

This is where the rubber meets the road. You must ask yourself how you will respond to the lesson.

Choose what you believe is the appropriate answer for you, and/or give an explanation of your answer in the space provided. Circle the answer where appropriate.

What do you feel is the greatest need in your life at this moment?
   More financial stability
   More friendships
   Freedom from addictions
   Greater education

_____

_____

Who is responsible for your recognizing the need to receive help for your addiction problems?
   You
   Family member
   Friend
   Coworker
   Other

_____

_____

Identify which group is your particular addiction behavior. Explain.
   Alcohol
   Drugs
   Pornography
   Gambling
   Combination of these

_____

_____

Do you believe your particular addiction behaviors have serious consequences?

Yes

No

_____

_____

**TRUE** or **FALSE**

Truth    Meter

Answer the following questions to the best of your ability. Some of these questions may be on the quiz at the end of the Pathway.

Please answer the following questions to the best of your ability. Write your answers in the spaces provided.

1. Nothing is more needful in the lives of people than to recognize they are _____ in need of the Saviour.

2. The world around us is in great turmoil and fear because of many _____.

3. _____ of people are quite literally being lost to addictions.

4. People with life-controlling habits can receive _____ recovery through a systematic learning of Biblical truths.

5. Addiction behaviors are _____ over the life cycle of the addiction.

6. The more prolonged the exposure to certain substances and activities, the more _____ the resulting behavior.

7. Many times, the addict's process of finding help is started by _____ other than himself.

8. Addiction to foods and other food related disorders do have _____ consequences.

9. Every aspect of the fruit of which Adam and Eve ate was very _____ to the flesh.

**Think about it!**

This area is for writing your thoughts and feelings about the information in this lesson. Please be honest with yourself. This exercise will help you understand and retain what you have read.

183

Thoughts and Feelings:

_____

_____

_____

_____

_____

_____

_____

_____

_____

_____

_____

Lesson Verse: Psalm 107:14

"He brought them out of darkness and the shadow of death, and brake their bands in sunder."

## Review

Choose what you believe is the appropriate answer for you, and/or give an explanation of your answer in the space provided. Circle the answer where appropriate.

184

Name some celebrities you are aware of through news and media that have had addiction problems.

_____
_____
_____

Explain which and how any of your family members have been affected by your addiction.

Parents

Spouse

Children

All

_____
_____

What kind of home environment do you desire to have? Why?

_____
_____
_____

Why do you think there are so many different rehab and recovery programs available throughout our country and even the world?

_____
_____

Is there anyone associated with you that you would consider to be a codependent? If yes, explain.

Yes

No

_____

_____

TRUE
or
FALSE
Truth ⬤ Meter

Answer the following questions to the best of your ability. Some of these questions may be on the quiz at the end of the Pathway.

Please answer the following questions to the best of your ability. Write your answers in the spaces provided.

1. Many _____ have been affected by the consequences of addictions.

2. Drug and alcohol addictions have been the cause of many _____ _____ of singers and actors over the years.

3. As society continues to search for the answer to addictions, Christians must continue to tell them the _____ in love.

4. Society will never find a cure for addiction while they look to ___ for the answer.

5. A _____ of our culture and society has taken place toward the things that were once unacceptable in public.

6. Many times _____ and separations occur because of addictions.

7. Addicts find themselves unable to sustain _____ for their addictions, especially in the later stages.

8. _____ is, when a person feels they are responsible for fixing the addict's condition.

9. Every person has the responsibility to be an _____ to other people of how to have faith in God.

186

**Think about it!**

This area is for writing your thoughts and feelings about the information in this lesson. Please be honest with yourself. This exercise will help you understand and retain what you have read.

Thoughts and Feelings:

_____

_____

_____

_____

_____

_____

_____

_____

_____

_____

**Lesson Verse: 1Peter2:21**

"For even hereunto were ye called: because Christ also suffered for us, leaving us an example, that ye should follow his steps:"

## Review

This is where the rubber meets the road. You must ask yourself how you will respond to the lesson.

Choose what you believe is the appropriate answer for you, and/or give an explanation of your answer in the space provided. Circle the answer where appropriate.

Describe, if any, a person whom you admired, that had an addiction problem.

_____

_____

_____

Before you began addiction behaviors, what was your honest opinion of people that had addiction problems?

_____

_____

Do you want to be free from the symptoms of your addiction, or the cause of your addiction? Why?

Symptoms

Cause

_____

_____

Describe, if any, a situation where you encountered a public humiliation as a direct result of your addiction.

_____

_____

TRUE or FALSE

Truth Meter

Answer the following questions to the best of your ability. Some of these questions may be on the quiz at the end of the Pathway.

Please answer the following questions to the best of your ability. Write your answers in the spaces provided.

1. Most everyone will, at some point in their life, encounter the _____ or consequences of a serious addiction problem, either directly or indirectly.

2. The problem of _____ in our society is much larger than most people are willing to admit.

3. The public believes whoever has the most _____ and can speak the loudest about addictions.

4. The world's answer to addictions is to treat the _____ of the problem and not the root cause of the problem.

5. The economic costs of substance abuse and addiction alone are estimated to exceed a half _____ dollars annually in the United States due to health care expenditures, lost productivity, and crime.

6. The number one health concern in America is _____ _____.

7. As humans, one of the ways in which we learn is through _____ we make that teach us how not to do something.

8. When the responsibility for addiction behaviors is removed from the addict and placed upon the idea that addiction is just a _____, the result is that the addict blames the _____.

**Think about it!**

This area is for writing your thoughts and feelings about the information in this lesson. Please be honest with yourself. This exercise will help you understand and retain what you have read.

Thoughts and Feelings:

_____

_____

_____

_____

_____

_____

_____

_____

_____

_____

**Lesson Verse: 1Timothy 5:20**

"Them that sin rebuke before all, that others also may fear."

## Review

This is where the rubber meets the road. You must ask yourself how you will respond to the lesson.

Choose what you believe is the appropriate answer for you, and/or give an explanation of your answer in the space provided. Circle the answer where appropriate.

Describe in what ways you feel your specific addiction has affected your community as a whole?

_____
_____
_____

Have you ever been in trouble with the law as a consequence of your addiction activities? If so, explain.

Yes

No

_____
_____

Explain why only participating in a detox program does not cure a person from their addiction.

_____
_____

Prior to starting this program, have you ever considered that addictions are sin?

Yes

No

Prior to starting this program, did you ever feel that an addiction was an illness? Why?

Yes

No

_____
_____

TRUE
or
FALSE

Truth ◯ Meter

Answer the following questions to the best of your ability. Some of these questions may be on the quiz at the end of the Pathway.

Please answer the following questions to the best of your ability. Write your answers in the spaces provided.

1. Sins of addiction diminish one's standing with their fellow man by failing to meet the _____ society has of its citizens.

2. Many times addicts are also on the wrong side of the law simply because of the _____ use of controlled substances.

3. The effects of addictions have reached into just about every _____ in America.

4. Our _____ spends millions of dollars each year combating the problem of addictions in our society.

5. The world's approach to addiction is to send the addict to the medical clinic or rehabilitation facility where the person "_____ ___"‖ or is "detached"‖ from the addiction for a period.

6. The _____ approach to addiction is to tell the truth in love. Addictions are sins.

7. The problem in the life of the addict is a ____ problem.

8. The cure for addictions lays in the fact that God _____ sin.

9. Sin is conquered by _____ and _____ in Jesus Christ for salvation, and a daily relationship with Him.

# PATHWAY 9 - Review Test

1. Satan deceived Eve into thinking she could satisfy her flesh, ignore the command of

   _____

2. God, and not suffer the _____ of that decision.

   _____

3. The most devastating effect addiction has on the individual is not the physical death; it is the _____ death of separation from God.

   _____

4. Satan's number one lie is that there is _____ to make things right with God.

   _____

5. The most common side effect of alcohol abuse is _____ of the liver.

   _____

6. We know that addictions are habits because they are _____ behaviors.

   _____

7. Habits are formed when a person repeatedly performs any behavior, whether good or bad (positive or negative), over a _____ _____.

   _____

8. The world around us is in great turmoil and fear because of many _____.

   _____

9. Society will never find a cure for addiction while they look to ___ for the answer.

   _____

# PATHWAY 10
# RECOVERY and RELAPSE

## MILSTONE 56

## ONE IN THE SAME

**Think about it!**

This area is for writing your thoughts and feelings about the information in this lesson. Please be honest with yourself. This exercise will help you understand and retain what you have read.

Thoughts and Feelings:

_____

_____

_____

_____

_____

_____

**Lesson Verse: Psalm 72:12**

"For he shall deliver the needy when he crieth; the poor also, and him that hath no helper. "

**Review**

This is where the rubber meets the road. You must ask yourself how you will respond to the lesson.

Choose what you believe is the appropriate answer for you, and/or give an explanation of your answer in the space provided. Circle the answer where appropriate.

**194**

Do you expect this program to give you the tools and information necessary to free you from your addiction? Why?

Yes

No

_____

_____

Describe, if any, a time when your addiction was treated with medication.

_____

_____

Explain why the cause of addictions should be addressed and not just the symptoms.

_____

_____

What do you understand the role of human nature to play in addiction behaviors?

_____

_____

Explain how a relationship with God can change the behaviors of a person in bondage to addictions.

_____

_____

TRUE
or
FALSE

Truth    Meter

Answer the following questions to the best of your ability. Some of these questions may be on the quiz at the end of the Pathway.

Please answer the following questions to the best of your ability. Write your answers in the spaces provided.

1. The most difficult task of an addiction recovery program is to give the addict _____ that will permanently deliver them from the clutches of an addiction.

2. There are support groups, therapy sessions, ongoing counseling, and a myriad of other post-rehab activities that have developed over the years, all for one reason - The problem of _____.

3. The solution can only be found in changing the person from the _____ out.

4. When we view addictions and the recovery process as two different issues, we inadvertently create a situation where recovery becomes the ____ of our programs.

5. When recovery becomes the goal of our programs, we place _____ on the addict that are unreasonable.

6. The ____ of relapse becomes the consuming emotion in the addict.

7. "For all have _____, and come short of the glory of God;"

8. Because God is merciful to us and has compassion toward us as His creations, we should also show _____ for one another.

9. Because God is _____, He forgives us every time we confess our sin to Him.

196

**Think about it!**

This area is for writing your thoughts and feelings about the information in this lesson. Please be honest with yourself. This exercise will help you understand and retain what you have read.

Thoughts and Feelings:

_____

_____

_____

_____

_____

_____

_____

_____

_____

_____

_____

**Lesson Verse: John 17:19**

*"And for their sakes I sanctify myself, that they also might be sanctified through the truth."*

## Review

Choose what you believe is the appropriate answer for you, and/or give an explanation of your answer in the space provided. Circle the answer where appropriate.

What do you believe are some of the traits of Christ that we should follow and emulate?

_____

_____

_____

What activities could we engage in that would help us become more like Christ?

_____

_____

Describe some traits in your life currently that would not be considered Christ-like.

_____

_____

Describe someone in your life that you feel is a good example of being Christ-like.

_____

_____

How much available time each day that could be spent reading and studying God's Word?

None

30 Minutes

1 Hour

2 Hours

_____

_____

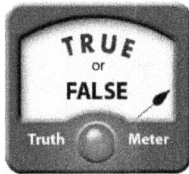

Answer the following questions to the best of your ability. Some of these questions may be on the quiz at the end of the Pathway.

Please answer the following questions to the best of your ability. Write your answers in the spaces provided.

198

1. Sanctification is the process God uses to produce _____ in the daily life of a person.

2. Sanctification is not accomplished in a set period, but in a _____.

3. The method God uses to accomplish this is reading, studying, memorizing, and _____ upon His Word, the Bible.

4. The same power that created the _____ and all that is in it, is the same power contained in the Word of God we hold in our hands.

5. We will stand in judgment of our deeds in the flesh, not for the _____ of sin.

6. The penalty of sin was paid for by _____ _____ on the cross of Calvary.

7. When we live a life that is Christ-like, we are able to lead _____ to the Saviour.

8. To be Christ-like, we need to study the Word of God and learn the traits of our _____, Jesus Christ.

9. Habits that reflect the nature of Christ are not created through the _____ of the individual.

10. Christ-likeness is produced by the _____ of the Holy Spirit as He changes the very nature and character of the person.

11. The process of sanctification is also a process of _____ in your spiritual life.

12. Spiritual _____ allows you to respond appropriately to circumstances and situations you are faced with in your daily life.

**Think about it!**

This area is for writing your thoughts and feelings about the information in this lesson. Please be honest with yourself. This exercise will help you understand and retain what you have read.

Thoughts and Feelings:

_____

_____

_____

_____

_____

_____

_____

_____

_____

_____

_____

**Lesson Verse: Proverbs 4:18**

"But the path of the just is as the shining light, that shineth more and more unto the perfect day."

## Review

This is where the rubber meets the road. You must ask yourself how you will respond to the lesson.

Choose what you believe is the appropriate answer for you, and/or give an explanation of your answer in the space provided. Circle the answer where appropriate.

200

Describe a time in your life where you may have gotten lost while driving or traveling.

_____
_____
_____

How did being lost make you feel?

_____
_____

Do you recognize that your addiction behaviors are sins? Explain.

Yes

No

_____
_____

Explain what it means for our sins to separate us from God.

_____
_____

**TRUE** or **FALSE**

Truth Meter

Answer the following questions to the best of your ability. Some of these questions may be on the quiz at the end of the Pathway.

Please answer the following questions to the best of your ability. Write your answers in the spaces provided.

1. Looking at addictions the way God looks at them is essential in _____ you from the bondage that holds you firmly in its grip.

2. God's way of dealing with sin in your life is for you to _____ of your sin and confess your sin to Him.

3. You do not deserve God's _____, but He extends it to you because of who He is, not because of who you are.

4. When you have a close relationship with Jesus Christ, and, by choice, you are living according to His commandments given in Scripture; recovery becomes a _____ of these actions.

5. The fear of relapse goes away because you recognize relapse as simply ___ _____ ___.

202

**Think about it!**

This area is for writing your thoughts and feelings about the information in this lesson. Please be honest with yourself. This exercise will help you understand and retain what you have read.

Thoughts and Feelings:

_____

_____

_____

_____

_____

_____

_____

_____

_____

_____

_____

**Lesson Verse: John 14:6**

"Jesus saith unto him, I am the way, the truth, and the life: no man cometh unto the Father, but by me."

# Review

This is where the rubber meets the road. You must ask yourself how you will respond to the lesson.

Choose what you believe is the appropriate answer for you, and/or give an explanation of your answer in the space provided. Circle the answer where appropriate.

What are some kinds of places that you should not frequent, so as to not be confronted with temptation for addiction behaviors?

_____

_____

_____

Describe some alternative activities that could replace your current addiction activities.

_____

_____

Recognizing that sanctification is a process, what do you feel needs to be removed from your life to allow this process to be as effective as possible?

_____

_____

Explain any fears you may have concerning your recovery process.

_____

_____

Describe some behaviors in your life, both destructive and constructive, that are similar but have very different consequences.

Destructive_____

_____

Constructive_____

_____

Please answer the following questions to the best of your ability. Write your answers in the spaces provided.

1.  Recovery can be understood as, a process of _____, which takes place over time.

2.  Sanctification is not an _____; it is a process.

3.  The Bible warns us against making an _____ to sin.

4.  Addicts should not place themselves in the position that encourages them to _____ God further.

5.  If the addict will live according to the Word of God, _____ will take care of itself.

6.  What a person does, in the eyes of God, is the most important way to view their _____.

7.  The right view of recovery is that we see the need for people to _____ Christ in obedience to God's Word each day.

8.  The right process begins with the _____ of a person's heart in salvation through our Lord Jesus Christ.

9.  The right process is: _____ to Jesus Christ.

10. Your future depends on your decision to take the right _____ toward Jesus Christ.

**Think about it!**

This area is for writing your thoughts and feelings about the information in this lesson. Please be honest with yourself. This exercise will help you understand and retain what you have read.

Thoughts and Feelings:

_____

_____

_____

_____

_____

_____

_____

_____

_____

_____

_____

**Lesson Verse: Ephesians 2:13**

"But now in Christ Jesus ye who sometimes were far off are made nigh by the blood of Christ."

## Review

This is where the rubber meets the road. You must ask yourself how you will respond to the lesson.

Choose what you believe is the appropriate answer for you, and/or give an explanation of your answer in the space provided. Circle the answer where appropriate.

What are some goals you have set in your life that you have already reached?

_____

_____

Name some goals you have set that you have not yet reached.

_____

_____

Explain why you feel it is important to set goals in your life.

_____

_____

At this point in your life, what would you say is the most important goal for you to reach?

_____

_____

How important to you is being right with God? Why?
   None
   Some
   Very
   Extremely

_____

_____

Describe some battles you have fought with your addiction, and won.

_____

_____

Please explain some current battles you are fighting with your addiction.

_____

_____

TRUE
or
FALSE

Truth  Meter

Answer the following questions to the best of your ability.
Some of these questions may be on the quiz at the end of the
Pathway.

Please answer the following questions to the best of your ability. Write your answers in the
spaces provided.

1. Becoming as much like Jesus Christ as possible in this flesh is the ____ of our
   efforts.

2. Because God is completely holy and righteous, He cannot allow us, in our sinful
   condition, into His _____.

3. When a person trusts Jesus Christ as their personal Saviour, and they are born into
   the family of God, they are given the _____ of Jesus Christ, God's Son.

4. "But God commendeth his love toward us, in that, while we were yet _____,
   Christ died for us."

5. In the typical addiction recovery program, _____ is the goal.

6. The right process is following the right _____, Jesus Christ.

208

**Think about it!**

This area is for writing your thoughts and feelings about the information in this lesson. Please be honest with yourself. This exercise will help you understand and retain what you have read.

Thoughts and Feelings:

_____

_____

_____

_____

_____

_____

_____

_____

_____

_____

_____

**Lesson Verse: Ecclesiastes 7:20**

"For there is not a just man upon the earth, that doeth good, and sinneth not."

## Review

This is where the rubber meets the road. You must ask yourself how you will respond to the lesson.

Choose what you believe is the appropriate answer for you, and/or give an explanation of your answer in the space provided. Circle the answer where appropriate.

Explain what you believe to be the meaning of relapse.

_____
_____
_____

Explain in your own words what it is like to be in fear of relapse.

_____
_____

How has the fear of relapse affected your actions or behaviors in the past?

_____
_____

What is the most dreaded part of the addiction, which you now have?

_____
_____

Including this program, how much money have you spent on all of your recovery efforts?

Less than $2000
Between $2000 and $5000
Between $5000 and $10,000
Over $10,000

_____
_____

Describe how it makes you feel that you have needed to spend this money on your recovery process.

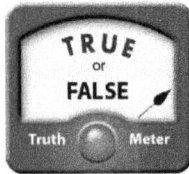

_____

_____

TRUE
or
FALSE

Truth  Meter

Answer the following questions to the best of your ability. Some of these questions may be on the quiz at the end of the Pathway.

Please answer the following questions to the best of your ability. Write your answers in the spaces provided.

1. _____ is simply a failure to live in obedience to God's Word.

2. I believe an addict should shoulder the _____ responsibility for their recovery process.

3. When the addict participates in the _____ of their recovery, this is taking responsibility for their own actions.

4. Relapse is an unrealistic measure of the _____ or failure of recovery programs.

5. A person who is trusting in Christ will rise up and continue through the power of God's _____.

6. The success of in a person's life should be determined by the measure of _____ visible in the life of that person over a period.

7. It is not _____ that make people what they are; it is circumstances that reveal the character of the person.

8. The main factors that determine the success of any particular program are the principles and tools given to the addict during the term of the program, and the _____ of the participant.

**Think about it!**

This area is for writing your thoughts and feelings about the information in this lesson. Please be honest with yourself. This exercise will help you understand and retain what you have read.

211

Thoughts and Feelings:

_____

_____

_____

_____

_____

_____

_____

_____

_____

_____

_____

**Lesson Verse: Ephesians 3:16**

"That he would grant you, according to the riches of his glory, to be strengthened with might by his Spirit in the inner man;"

## Review

This is where the rubber meets the road. You must ask yourself how you will respond to the lesson.

Choose what you believe is the appropriate answer for you, and/or give an explanation of your answer in the space provided. Circle the answer where appropriate.

How many drug rehab and residential facilities are there in your surrounding area?

No idea

Less than 10

More than 10

More than 50

How many of these are "faith-based" programs?

_____

Explain what it means to you to have your heart changed, as opposed to your environment.

_____

_____

Have you ever been incarcerated long-term, as a result of your addiction behaviors? Explain.

Yes

No

_____

_____

Explain in your own words what you believe the text is trying to say regarding how an addiction recovery program should present the Gospel.

_____

_____

Have you made the decision to have a specific time each day to read the Bible and pray? Explain.

Yes

No

_____

_____

213

Answer the following questions to the best of your ability. Some of these questions may be on the quiz at the end of the Pathway.

Please answer the following questions to the best of your ability. Write your answers in the spaces provided.

1. It is the _____ of a person that causes him to either obey or disobey the laws of God and man.

2. Ministry-based programs have a great opportunity to make a difference in our _____ now.

3. There is a tremendous need for many more church _____ in this field.

4. _____ are at an all-time high. It will be the local churches that make a lasting

5. It is the power of the Word of God that _____ a life.

6. There must be _____ and wisdom used in how we present the truths of God's Word to the addict.

7. Most addicts are _____ and have a low tolerance for pain.

8. The addict's _____ can also make it very difficult for them to perform even normal logical thought processes.

9.  The same gospel that speaks to the hearts of everyone is the gospel the ____ _____ will use in the life of the addict to bring them to Christ.

10. Experience has proven that when a clear foundation of basic truths is laid prior to presenting the gospel, there is more _____ and openness to the gospel on the part of the addict.

# PATHWAY 10 - Review Test

1. "For all have _____, and come short of the glory of God;"

_____

2. The solution can only be found in changing the person from the _____ out.

_____

3. Sanctification is the process God uses to produce _____ in the daily life of a person.

_____

4. The penalty of sin was paid for by _____ _____ on the cross of Calvary.

_____

5. Spiritual _____ allows you to respond appropriately to circumstances and situations you are faced with in your daily life.

_____

6. The fear of relapse goes away because you recognize relapse as simply ___ _____ ___.

_____

7. Sanctification is not an _____; it is a process.

_____

8. If the addict will live according to the Word of God, _____ will take care of itself.

_____

9. "But God commendeth his love toward us, in that, while we were yet _____,

Christ died for us."

_____

## MILSTONE 63
## THE IMPORTANCE OF BELIEF

**Think about it!**

This area is for writing your thoughts and feelings about the information in this lesson. Please be honest with yourself. This exercise will help you understand and retain what you have read.

Thoughts and Feelings:

_____

_____

_____

_____

_____

_____

**Lesson Verse: Mark 9:23**

"Jesus said unto him, If thou canst believe, all things are possible to him that believeth."

## Review

This is where the rubber meets the road. You must ask yourself how you will respond to the lesson.

Choose what you believe is the appropriate answer for you, and/or give an explanation of your answer in the space provided. Circle the answer where appropriate.

As a result of taking this course thus far, what are some behaviors that you now recognize as being addiction behaviors that you did not recognize before?

_____

_____

If any, what do you believe has been the basis for your belief system?

_____

_____

What would you say is your philosophy of life?

_____

_____

Explain in your own words how our human nature affects our actions and behaviors.

_____

_____

**TRUE or FALSE**

Truth Meter

Answer the following questions to the best of your ability. Some of these questions may be on the quiz at the end of the Pathway.

Please answer the following questions to the best of your ability. Write your answers in the spaces provided.

1. Belief – A persuasion of truth on the grounds of _____ distinct from personal knowledge.

2. System – Regular union of _____ or parts forming one entire thing; regular method or order.

3. Way of life – Behavior based upon patterns of _____; routine actions based upon a series of accepted principles or theories.

4. A Belief System is a _____ of principles that determine our response to any circumstance we face in life.

5. The belief system to which we adhere determines the _____ we make.

6. Having the wrong belief system allows a person to make decisions that are _____ to the laws and commands of God.

7. If a person has no _____ for belief or a specific set of values, they will in turn believe anything and any behavior will be acceptable to them.

8. Man's actions must be guided by an established set of _____ values or chaos and violence will result.

9. What a person _____ determines how they live.

10. What a person believes about ___ will determine what they believe to be the meaning of life.

11. _____ is the study of who God is.

12. What a person understands or believes about God, because of what he thinks he knows to be true about God, is called _____.

13. Many people construct their philosophy for life from their _____.

14. The secure way to construct a strong philosophy is to base our philosophy of life on a _____ that does not change.

15. The only standard that does not change is ___.

16. _____ is a very powerful tool in the process of recovery from life-controlling habits and behaviors.

# WHERE BELIEF BEGINS

**Think about it!**

This area is for writing your thoughts and feelings about the information in this lesson. Please be honest with yourself. This exercise will help you understand and retain what you have read.

219

Thoughts and Feelings:

_____

_____

_____

_____

_____

_____

_____

_____

_____

_____

**Lesson Verse: John 3:17**

"For God sent not his Son into the world to condemn the world; but that the world through him might be saved."

## Review

220

This is where the rubber meets the road. You must ask yourself how you will respond to the lesson.

Choose what you believe is the appropriate answer for you, and/or give an explanation of your answer in the space provided. Circle the answer where appropriate.

What do you believe is your current level of self-esteem?
Poor
Average
High

_____
_____

Explain in your own words the meaning of receiving a "gift."

_____
_____

Explain what you believe it means to be "made the righteousness of God" by Jesus Christ.

_____
_____

Have you ever been afraid to "not go to meetings?" Why?
Yes
No

_____
_____

Why is it important that we know the truth about any matter?

_____
_____

TRUE or FALSE

Truth | Meter

Answer the following questions to the best of your ability. Some of these questions may be on the quiz at the end of the Pathway.

Please answer the following questions to the best of your ability. Write your answers in the spaces provided.

1.  You must see ____ as the greatest problem in your life, and the root cause of all addictions.

2.  Our society has placed such a premium on _____ and self-esteem many people no longer feel any need to admit that they are a sinner in need of the Saviour.

3.  No one wants to be _____ with the prospect of being sinful.

4.  Our society blames addictions on a _____ or illness.

5.  Society says it is the "disease" of addiction that forces a person to _____ the lusts of the flesh.

6.  God convicts us of our sin because He _____ us.

7.  By accepting Jesus Christ as our Saviour, we have the same _____ over sin and death that Jesus has.

8.  The freedom we have in Christ is as _____ as God is; it is as complete as is the plan of salvation itself.

9.  A person controlled by drugs or alcohol is a _____ to and in bondage to sins.

10. If a person must go to meetings in order to stay clean or sober I would submit to you that, they are simply trading one life-controlling habit or _____ for another.

11. God forgives us each time we _____ our sin.

12. Not only does God forgive us of our sins, but also once they are under the blood, He does not _____ them any longer.

222

**Think about it!**

This area is for writing your thoughts and feelings about the information in this lesson. Please be honest with yourself. This exercise will help you understand and retain what you have read.

Thoughts and Feelings:

_____

_____

_____

_____

_____

_____

_____

_____

_____

_____

_____

**Lesson Verse: Proverbs 1:8**

"My son, hear the instruction of thy father, and forsake not the law of thy mother:"

## Review

Choose what you believe is the appropriate answer for you, and/or give an explanation of your answer in the space provided. Circle the answer where appropriate.

What person or group of people had the most influence on you as a young child?

_____

_____

Explain the level of instruction about God that you received as a young person.
    None
    Some
    Much

_____

_____

From where did you receive the most instruction?
    Home
    School
    Church
    Other

_____

_____

Have you ever viewed yourself as a victim of society?
    Yes
    No

_____

_____

Describe the grace of God, as you understand it.

_____

_____

Please answer the following questions to the best of your ability. Write your answers in the spaces provided.

1. The concept a person has of God is created by _____ influences and will determine a person's belief system.

2. An incorrect _____ with authority figures can affect that person's relationship with God.

3. The relationship a person has with their parents or those who rear them is one of the most powerful factors that shape a person's _____ of God and their ability to relate to others.

4. The type of authority a person has in their early childhood development also contributes a great deal in _____ many other aspects of their thinking.

5. The Home, School, Church, and community are some of the most common sources of _____ early in a person's life.

6. The _____ is the most influential place of instruction in the early years of a person's life.

7. Most family members are trusted to do what is right, but they do not always do what is _____.

8. The community many times looks to the _____ leaders as examples they want their children to follow.

9. The greater the degree of guilt, the greater the amount of blame placed on other people and _____.

10. The Bible gives us examples of how sin can take _____ of a person.

11. Grace is God's unmerited _____ on our lives.

12. The right concept of God allows us to see Him as the ultimate _____ in our life.

13. God's ____ never changes.

14. Our life is either an example for others to follow or an _____ for others to copy.

15. It is through obedient living that we bring _____ to God.

226

**Think about it!**

This area is for writing your thoughts and feelings about the information in this lesson. Please be honest with yourself. This exercise will help you understand and retain what you have read.

Thoughts and Feelings:

_____

_____

_____

_____

_____

_____

_____

_____

_____

_____

_____

**Lesson Verse: Proverbs 22:28**

"Remove not the ancient landmark, which thy fathers have set."

## Review

This is where the rubber meets the road. You must ask yourself how you will respond to the lesson.

Choose what you believe is the appropriate answer for you, and/or give an explanation of your answer in the space provided. Circle the answer where appropriate.

Give a brief statement concerning what you believe about God.

_____
_____
_____
_____

Describe what you believe about creation.

_____
_____

Explain what you believe your purpose in life to be.

_____
_____

Briefly describe what it means to be accountable to God.

_____
_____

In your own words, tell why it is important to receive instruction.

_____
_____

Explain why it is important that we all learn to be obedient to those that have authority over us.

_____
_____

How does our position in God relate to the addiction recovery process?

_____

_____

TRUE
or
FALSE

Truth        Meter

Answer the following questions to the best of your ability. Some of these questions may be on the quiz at the end of the Pathway.

Please answer the following questions to the best of your ability. Write your answers in the spaces provided.

1. Having the proper concept of God determines the _____ _____ we will have.

2. "Keep thy heart with all diligence; for out of it are the _____ of life."

3. What we believe about God determines what we believe about _____.

4. If there is no purpose for having been created, we will not believe we are _____ to God.

5. Instability and uncertainty prevents a person from understanding the _____ they have as God's most celebrated and important creation.

6. Not understanding our worth as God's creation, prevents a person from understanding our _____ to God.

7. The absence of Biblical _____ and role models in the life of an addict contributes to having the wrong concept of God.

8. When a person believes in God, they also believe God _____ them.

9. If God created a person for a reason, then that person is accountable to God for that _____.

**Think about it!**

This area is for writing your thoughts and feelings about the information in this lesson. Please be honest with yourself. This exercise will help you understand and retain what you have read.

229

Thoughts and Feelings:

_____
_____
_____
_____
_____
_____
_____
_____
_____
_____
_____

**Lesson Verse: Romans 1:19**

"Because that which may be known of God is manifest in them; for God hath shewed it unto them."

## Review

This is where the rubber meets the road. You must ask yourself how you will respond to the lesson.

Choose what you believe is the appropriate answer for you, and/or give an explanation of your answer in the space provided. Circle the answer where appropriate.

230

Describe a time in your life when you were the happiest.

_____
_____
_____

Briefly contrast the happiest time in your life with your current circumstances.

_____
_____

In what ways have your addiction controlled your life?

_____
_____

Explain the similarities between what you are experiencing as a result of your addiction and what other addicts you know also face.

_____
_____

What is your level of desire to be free from the bondage addiction? Explain.
Weak
Medium
Strong

_____
_____

Answer the following questions to the best of your ability. Some of these questions may be on the quiz at the end of the Pathway.

Please answer the following questions to the best of your ability. Write your answers in the spaces provided.

1.  A person either forms a belief system based upon what they think they know, or from an _____.

2.  Human beings must receive clear _____ from God to have a correctly constructed belief system.

3.  _____ is not found in fulfilling the desires of one's self; it is in fulfilling the desires of the Creator.

4.  Man was made to _____ with the Creator.

5.  The only way man can have fellowship with the Creator is to be obedient to the Creator's _____.

6.  In a _____ society, there is no concept of God or one's responsibility to Him.

7.  No one can free _____ from the bondage of addiction.

8.  Men do not want to be accountable to a holy and righteous God, so they _____ to not understand anything about God.

# PATHWAY 11 - Review Test

1. A Belief System is a _____ of principles that determine our response to any circumstance we face in life.

_____

2. The belief system to which we adhere determines the _____ we make.

_____

3. The only standard that does not change is ___.

_____

4. What a person _____ determines how they live.

_____

5. You must see ___ as the greatest problem in your life, and the root cause of all addictions.

_____

6. Our society blames addictions on a _____ or illness.

_____

7. God forgives us each time we _____ our sin.

_____

8. An incorrect _____ with authority figures can affect that person's relationship with God.

_____

9. The ____ is the most influential place of instruction in the early years of a person's life.

_____

10. Grace is God's unmerited _____ on our lives.

_____

# PATHWAY 12
# CHOICES

## MILSTONE 68
## HOW WE CHOOSE

**Think about it!**

This area is for writing your thoughts and feelings about the information in this lesson. Please be honest with yourself. This exercise will help you understand and retain what you have read.

Thoughts and Feelings:

_____

_____

_____

_____

_____

_____

**Lesson Verse: Joshua 24:15a**

"And if it seem evil unto you to serve the LORD, choose you this day whom ye will serve;"

## Review

This is where the rubber meets the road. You must ask yourself how you will respond to the lesson.

Choose what you believe is the appropriate answer for you, and/or give an explanation of your answer in the space provided. Circle the answer where appropriate.

234

Describe how you made the choice to start down the path to addiction behaviors.

_____

_____

Explain the differences in our body, our soul and our spirit, as you understand them.

_____

_____

_____

_____

What does the term "eternal life" mean to you?

_____

_____

Explain what you believe to be the definition of an "objective standard."

_____

_____

Give some examples of a "subjective reasoning" decisions.

_____

_____

TRUE
or
FALSE

Truth   Meter

Answer the following questions to the best of your ability. Some of these questions may be on the quiz at the end of the Pathway.

Please answer the following questions to the best of your ability. Write your answers in the spaces provided.

1. The choices we make in our life affect how we live our life now and where we will live after _____.

2. We must have a fixed point of _____ by which to make our choices and decisions.

3. God has given us a fixed point of reference. It is the _____ Word of God.

4. Man was created in the _____ and likeness of God.

5. Man has a _____ and spirit not just a body.

6. The most important revelation of _____ is found in the person of Jesus Christ.

7. Jesus Christ is _____.

236

**Think about it!**

This area is for writing your thoughts and feelings about the information in this lesson. Please be honest with yourself. This exercise will help you understand and retain what you have read.

Thoughts and Feelings:

_____

_____

_____

_____

_____

_____

_____

_____

_____

_____

_____

Lesson Verse: Proverbs 27:17

"Iron sharpeneth iron; so a man sharpeneth the countenance of his friend."

**Review**

This is where the rubber meets the road. You must ask yourself how you will respond to the lesson.

Choose what you believe is the appropriate answer for you, and/or give an explanation of your answer in the space provided. Circle the answer where appropriate.

Describe the kind of influence you desire to be toward your friends and family.

_____

_____

_____

Describe how you believe your life has influenced others up to this point in your life.

_____

_____

What kind of person do you desire this addiction recovery program to help you become?

_____

_____

How many people do you know that you would consider being a "true" friend to you? Why?

_____

_____

Describe a circumstance where you were either abandoned or betrayed by a friend.

_____

_____

**TRUE or FALSE**

Truth Meter

Answer the following questions to the best of your ability. Some of these questions may be on the quiz at the end of the Pathway.

Please answer the following questions to the best of your ability. Write your answers in the spaces provided.

1. We all have the responsibility of recognizing how our _____ and choices affect other people.

2. The choices you make for yourself will determine if your life will _____ others for good or for evil.

3. God will hold us personally responsible for the _____ in which we influence others.

4. Our choice of how our life will affect others begins with our ____.

5. You should look for people that will kindly tell you the _____ about yourself.

6. _____ friends will help you become all that God intends for you to be.

7. Ungodly friends are really not you friends because they only want what _____ them in the long run.

8. Someone that always tells you what you want to hear is either trying to ____ you something or ____ something away from you.

9. God _____ you enough to send you the right kind of people to be your friends.

**Think about it!**

This area is for writing your thoughts and feelings about the information in this lesson. Please be honest with yourself. This exercise will help you understand and retain what you have read.

239

Thoughts and Feelings:

_____
_____
_____
_____
_____
_____
_____
_____
_____
_____
_____

**Lesson Verse: 2Timothy 3:7**

"Ever learning, and never able to come to the knowledge of the truth."

## Review

> This is where the rubber meets the road. You must ask yourself how you will respond to the lesson.

Choose what you believe is the appropriate answer for you, and/or give an explanation of your answer in the space provided. Circle the answer where appropriate.

Describe a situation where a negative choice affected you in a physical way.

_____

_____

Describe a situation where a negative choice affected you in an emotional way.

_____

_____

Explain in your own words what you believe to be the main difference in secular addiction recovery programs and Christian-based programs.

_____

_____

What do you feel is the greatest choice you could make in your life at the moment?

_____

_____

TRUE
or
FALSE

Truth      Meter

> Answer the following questions to the best of your ability. Some of these questions may be on the quiz at the end of the Pathway.

Please answer the following questions to the best of your ability. Write your answers in the spaces provided.

1. Practically every addict's _____ condition is the result of poor choices.

2. Instead of clamoring for the high pedestal of _____, we choose to acknowledge the truth about why people make poor choices.

3. People make negative choices because they are not led by _____ knowledge and obedience.

4. The problem with addiction activities is that the activity is, more than not, a result of selfish desire to gratify one's flesh as a result of man's _____ _____.

5. Because man always thinks he can _____ on God, he resists any notion that reminds him of his finite and frail existence.

242

**Think about it!**

This area is for writing your thoughts and feelings about the information in this lesson. Please be honest with yourself. This exercise will help you understand and retain what you have read.

Thoughts and Feelings:

_____

_____

_____

_____

_____

_____

_____

_____

_____

_____

_____

_____

**Lesson Verse: Psalm 119:9**

"Wherewithal shall a young man cleanse his way? by taking heed thereto according to thy word."

## Review

This is where the rubber meets the road. You must ask yourself how you will respond to the lesson.

Choose what you believe is the appropriate answer for you, and/or give an explanation of your answer in the space provided. Circle the answer where appropriate.

Are you willing to do whatever it takes to be free from your addiction bondage? Why?

Yes

No

_____

_____

Describe a situation where a positive choice resulted in a positive outcome.

_____

_____

What do you expect this program to help you accomplish? Be specific.

_____

_____

Describe by what method or criteria you decide if a particular choice is good or bad.

_____

_____

Describe the best job you ever had. Explain why.

_____

_____

Would you say you have a temporal view of life or an eternal view? Why?

Temporal

Eternal

_____

_____

Answer the following questions to the best of your ability. Some of these questions may be on the quiz at the end of the Pathway.

Please answer the following questions to the best of your ability. Write your answers in the spaces provided.

1. What you expect from _____ while taking this course is a reflection of how serious you are about your recovery process and just how tired you are of being controlled by your addiction.

2. The greatest challenge in making decisions is, not making the choice between right and wrong, or good and bad, but making the choice between good and ____.

3. Choosing between good and best is more difficult because they both are good and can be _____.

4. God gives us _____ to know the difference when we read and study His Word every day and spend time with Him in prayer.

5. As we grow in the Lord, He gives us _____ into the truth and how to know truth from error.

6. This ability comes only from ___ and is essential in making the right choices for your life.

# SOWING AND REAPING

**Think about it!**

This area is for writing your thoughts and feelings about the information in this lesson. Please be honest with yourself. This exercise will help you understand and retain what you have read.

Thoughts and Feelings:

_____

_____

_____

_____

_____

_____

_____

_____

_____

_____

_____

**Lesson Verse: Galatians 6:7**

"Be not deceived; God is not mocked: for whatsoever a man soweth, that shall he also reap."

**Review**

Choose what you believe is the appropriate answer for you, and/or give an explanation of your answer in the space provided. Circle the answer where appropriate.

Explain your understanding of the meaning of sowing and reaping.

_____

_____

_____

What kind of life do you desire to live for the rest of your time on this earth?

_____

_____

Based on the previous question's answer, explain why.

_____

_____

What do you feel the results would be of you continuing in the direction you are now headed? Why?

_____

_____

Considering the law of sowing and reaping, describe some positive things that you would like to reap in your life.

_____

_____

What, in your life, do you believe will have to change, in order to reap the positive things given in the previous answer?

_____

_____

TRUE
or
FALSE
Truth ⬤ Meter

Answer the following questions to the best of your ability. Some of these questions may be on the quiz at the end of the Pathway.

Please answer the following questions to the best of your ability. Write your answers in the spaces provided.

1. _____ Laws are laws to which all mankind must answer, regardless of any differences in race, religion, creed, social status, financial standing, political affiliation, ancestry or beliefs about God.

2. In His Word, God has given you all the _____ you need for you to know how to make the right choices in your life.

3. You must decide what you want for the rest of your life on this earth, and what you want for your life throughout _____.

4. Understanding the law of _____ and reaping will help you make choices that result in benefits and blessings instead of sorrow and suffering.

5. The law of sowing and reaping should never be viewed solely as an instrument of _____ feedback.

6. You should look at the law of sowing and reaping as an opportunity to make _____ things happen for you.

7. The Bible states that when you sow to the flesh, you will, "of the flesh reap _____."

8. Regardless if you sow addiction behaviors of drug abuse, alcohol abuse, food or tobacco, the resulting _____ is a diminished body and spirit.

9. As you start the physical healing process, you will find that your mental and _____ well-being will also increase.

# PATHWAY 12 - Review Test

1. The choices we make in our life affect how we live our life now and where we will live after _____.

_____

2. Man was created in the _____ and likeness of God.

_____

3. We all have the responsibility of recognizing how our _____ and choices affect other people.

_____

4. You should look for people that will kindly tell you the _____ about yourself.

_____

5. _____ friends will help you become all that God intends for you to be.

_____

6. Practically every addict's _____ condition is the result of poor choices.

_____

7. People make negative choices because they are not led by _____ knowledge and obedience.

_____

8. Choosing between good and best is more difficult because they both are good and can be _____.

_____

9. God gives us _____ to know the difference when we read and study His Word every day and spend time with Him in prayer.

_____

# PATHWAY 13
# THE CURE

## MILSTONE 73
## ADMITTING THE CURE

**Think about it!**

This area is for writing your thoughts and feelings about the information in this lesson. Please be honest with yourself. This exercise will help you understand and retain what you have read.

Thoughts and Feelings:

_____
_____
_____
_____
_____
_____

**Lesson Verse: Philippians 2:5**

**"Let this mind be in you, which was also in Christ Jesus:"**

## Review

This is where the rubber meets the road. You must ask yourself how you will respond to the lesson.

Choose what you believe is the appropriate answer for you, and/or give an explanation of your answer in the space provided. Circle the answer where appropriate.

Do you feel your addiction behaviors are inappropriate? Explain.

Yes

No

_____

_____

Have you ever encountered the idea that you have the power to control and remove addictions from yourself? Explain.

Yes

No

_____

_____

Explain in your own words the difference in the old nature of man and the new nature that God gives him.

_____

_____

_____

What does it mean to you for a person to be "spiritual?"

_____

_____

Explain what it means to you to be secure.

_____

_____

Explain the level of emotional security you feel you have at this time in your life.
Low
Average
High

_____

_____

TRUE
or
FALSE
Truth  Meter

Answer the following questions to the best of your ability.
Some of these questions may be on the quiz at the end of the
Pathway.

Please answer the following questions to the best of your ability. Write your answers in the
spaces provided.

1. The root problem of addiction is the _____ nature of all human beings.

2. The best result obtained through a humanistic program is a marginal _____ of
   the outward behaviors and activities of the addict.

3. None of us has the _____ within ourselves to overcome life-controlling habits
   permanently.

4. We must combat our sinful nature every day, and we simply do not have the strength
   or power within ourselves to resist the _____ of our flesh.

5. Some people are strong emotionally and have a measure of _____ to control
   certain desires, but in the end, the flesh will win.

6. _____ is a process of permanent outward change that takes place over
   time, originating from a supernatural change in man's heart by God.

7. The only way to be transformed by the renewing of our mind is through a
   _____ work of God on the inside of a person.

8. God performs this supernatural change in us as we accept _____ _____ as our
   personal Saviour.

9. God gives us a new _____ in Christ, and a new nature.

10. The desire to have the _____ of Christ is one of the things God gives us when we receive the new nature mentioned in 2Corinthians 5:17-18.

11. Because we now have two natures, there is a tremendous _____ that takes place between our old nature and our new nature.

12. For the new man to ___ the struggles, we must feed the mind with things of God and not things of the flesh.

13. Counsel and restoration go hand-in-hand, but _____ is postponed or stifled when we fall into the trap of prolonged counseling sessions.

14. _____ counseling sessions inadvertently teach the addict to rely upon himself to correct the problems in his life.

15. It is the Word of God and the power of the _____ presence of the Holy Spirit that changes the heart of men, and therefore, their actions, not our ideas and formulas.

**Think about it!**

This area is for writing your thoughts and feelings about the information in this lesson. Please be honest with yourself. This exercise will help you understand and retain what you have read.

253

Thoughts and Feelings:

_____

_____

_____

_____

_____

_____

_____

_____

_____

_____

_____

**Lesson Verse: 1John 4:4**

"Ye are of God, little children, and have overcome them; because greater is he that is in you, than he that is in the world."

## Review

This is where the rubber meets the road. You must ask yourself how you will respond to the lesson.

Choose what you believe is the appropriate answer for you, and/or give an explanation of your answer in the space provided. Circle the answer where appropriate.

Explain what you believe to be "spiritual" death.

_____

_____

_____

Have you ever trusted in Jesus Christ as your personal Lord and Saviour? Explain.
Yes
No

_____

_____

If you have not, would you like to know how to trust in Jesus Christ now?
Yes
No

If you answered yes to the previous question, let your Sponsor or you Professor know that you desire to accept Christ as your Saviour, then answer yes or no to the following question.

Have you contacted your Sponsor or Professor to let them know you desire to trust in Jesus Christ?
Yes
No

_____

_____

Answer the following questions to the best of your ability. Some of these questions may be on the quiz at the end of the Pathway.

Please answer the following questions to the best of your ability. Write your answers in the spaces provided.

1. It is our nature to do wrong and make bad choices, but it is also God's _____ that we do right.

2. We cannot do right in our _____, but we can do right living in the new life that Christ gives.

3. "Therefore if any man be in Christ, he is a new _____: old things are passed away; behold, all things are become new."

4. The Holy Spirit reveals the _____ of God's Word to us, and the understanding of God's Word enables us to know what is right.

5. When we accept Jesus Christ, God's Son, as our Saviour, God then takes the spotless record of His Son Jesus and applies it to our record as though we were never a _____.

6. _____ has never helped a person find true freedom from sin.

7. Religion only soothes the _____ of man for a short period.

8. _____ only places men in further bondage.

9. "To Reach and Restore" should be the _____ of every Christian.

10. We must love the _____ before we can love the ones whom the Saviour loves.

256

**Think about it!**

This area is for writing your thoughts and feelings about the information in this lesson. Please be honest with yourself. This exercise will help you understand and retain what you have read.

Thoughts and Feelings:

_____

_____

_____

_____

_____

_____

_____

_____

_____

_____

_____

_____

Lesson Verse: John 15:5b

"...for without me ye can do nothing."

## Review

This is where the rubber meets the road. You must ask yourself how you will respond to the lesson.

Choose what you believe is the appropriate answer for you, and/or give an explanation of your answer in the space provided. Circle the answer where appropriate.

Name a few good examples of the right kind of pride.

_____

_____

_____

What are some examples of the wrong kind of pride?

_____

_____

Describe any addiction recovery programs that you have attended in the past.

_____

_____

_____

Do you recognize that God is the only Person who can free you from your addiction?
Yes
No

How willing are you to allow God to change your behaviors?
None
Some
Very

_____

_____

Answer the following questions to the best of your ability. Some of these questions may be on the quiz at the end of the Pathway.

Please answer the following questions to the best of your ability. Write your answers in the spaces provided.

258

1. Most recovery programs do not understand the _____ of addictions.

2. I do not believe a _____ approach to recovery is the correct approach.

3. The Word of God is the source of education and _____ for the addiction recovery ministry.

4. We have tried to "understand"‖ rather than _____.

5. We have brushed aside the sin and focused on the need to be esteemed through new and more _____ competencies.

6. We have forgotten that men are _____ and need the Saviour.

7. _____ our pride also means that you must admit that you need help.

8. The wrong kind of pride prevents a person from recognizing the need of their life and allowing the real _____ to their life-controlling habit to take effect.

9. A _____ person will also blame others for their indiscretions and mistakes.

10. The only way to remove pride from our hearts is to _____ it to God and allow the Holy Spirit to teach us humility.

Think about it!

This area is for writing your thoughts and feelings about the information in this lesson. Please be honest with yourself. This exercise will help you understand and retain what you have read.

Thoughts and Feelings:

_____

_____

_____

_____

_____

_____

_____

_____

_____

_____

_____

**Lesson Verse: Psalm 119:105**

**"Thy word is a lamp unto my feet, and a light unto my path."**

## Review

Choose what you believe is the appropriate answer for you, and/or give an explanation of your answer in the space provided. Circle the answer where appropriate.

How important do you believe God's Word is to your personal recovery process?
    None
    Some
    Very

_____

_____

Do you believe there is life after death? Why
    Yes
    No

_____

_____

What do you believe to be the best preparation for eternity? Why?

_____

_____

How many, if any, "drying out" programs have you attended personally?
    None
    One
    More than 2
    More than 5

_____

_____

Do you feel you are the kind of person that recognizes the truth when you see it?
    Yes
    Maybe

**TRUE or FALSE**

Truth — Meter

Answer the following questions to the best of your ability. Some of these questions may be on the quiz at the end of the Pathway.

Please answer the following questions to the best of your ability. Write your answers in the spaces provided.

1. God's Word gives us the _____ to deal with human nature correctly.

2. The _____ approach is much more effective, and costs far less money to operate than do government intervention programs.

3. The _____ approach is the only program that has the ability to transform a person from the inside out.

4. Without the internal change happening within a person, there will not be a _____ recovery.

5. Anything that helps a person be _____ in society has value to that society.

6. There is life after death, and there is a _____ God to whom we all will have to give an answer.

7. Being right with God means a person can live in the _____ of God's blessings, both in this life and in the life hereafter.

8. It takes more than programs, facilities, and "drying" a person out, to effectively help them obtain lasting _____ from the bondage of addictions.

9. There must be a daily _____ to a relationship with Jesus Christ.

10. Recovery takes place as the participant reads, studies, and _____ Scripture.

# PATHWAY 13 - Review Test

1. The root problem of addiction is the _____ nature of all human beings.

_____

2. The only way to be transformed by the renewing of our mind is through a _____ work of God on the inside of a person.

_____

3. Because we now have two natures, there is a tremendous _____ that takes place between our old nature and our new nature.

_____

4. "Therefore if any man be in Christ, he is a new _____: old things are passed away; behold, all things are become new."

_____

5. Religion only soothes the _____ of man for a short period.

_____

6. The Word of God is the source of education and _____ for the addiction recovery ministry.

_____

7. A _____ person will also blame others for their indiscretions and mistakes.

_____

8. God's Word gives us the _____ to deal with human nature correctly.

_____

9. Recovery takes place as the participant reads, studies, and _____ Scripture.

_____

# PATHWAY 14
# RELATIONSHIPS

## MILSTONE 77
## FAMILY AND FRIENDS

**Think about it!**

This area is for writing your thoughts and feelings about the information in this lesson. Please be honest with yourself. This exercise will help you understand and retain what you have read.

Thoughts and Feelings:

_____

_____

_____

_____

_____

_____

Lesson verse: Galatians 6:10

"As we have therefore opportunity, let us do good unto all men, especially unto them who are of the household of faith."

**Review**

This is where the rubber meets the road. You must ask yourself how you will respond to the lesson.

Choose what you believe is the appropriate answer for you, and/or give an explanation of your answer in the space provided. Circle the answer where appropriate.

At this time in your life, what is the most important relationship you have? Why?

_____

_____

Describe some of the expectations you have of your family members.

_____

_____

What are some expectations your family members have of you?

_____

_____

How would you describe the manner in which the majority of your friends and family responded to your addiction?

    Apathetically

    Compassionately

    Angrily

    Confusion

_____

_____

Explain how your addiction has completely destroyed a relationship, if any.

_____

_____

Answer the following questions to the best of your ability. Some of these questions may be on the quiz at the end of the Pathway.

Please answer the following questions to the best of your ability. Write your answers in the spaces provided.

1. Other than the relationship we have with the Lord Jesus, the most important relationships we can have are with _____ and friends.

2. Relationships with family and friends can definitely be some of the most _____ and challenging relationships we have.

3. If a family member or friend is strong emotionally or mature _____, they will respond with love and understanding to the addict's needs and behaviors.

4. The spiritually mature family member or friend will not supply the addict with _____ or means whereby the addict can perpetuate their addiction.

5. The spiritually mature Christian realizes the needs of the addict and will try and help the addict make decisions toward a _____ recovery.

6. Family and friends are important to the _____ process.

7. You have a responsibility toward your family and friends to recognize any areas where you may have _____ your relationship.

8. Sin always _____.

9. Most addicts destroy their relationship with family and friends early in the addiction cycle because these people are the _____ to them.

10. You should recognize that if you still have a relationship with family or friends, it is a _____ from God.

266

**Think about it!**

This area is for writing your thoughts and feelings about the information in this lesson. Please be honest with yourself. This exercise will help you understand and retain what you have read.

Thoughts and Feelings:

_____
_____
_____
_____
_____
_____
_____
_____
_____
_____
_____

Lesson Verse: 2Timothy 2:22

"Flee also youthful lusts: but follow righteousness, faith, charity, peace, with them that call on the Lord out of a pure heart."

# Review

This is where the rubber meets the road. You must ask yourself how you will respond to the lesson.

Choose what you believe is the appropriate answer for you, and/or give an explanation of your answer in the space provided. Circle the answer where appropriate.

(Please be appropriate with all answers in this section. Thank you.)

Discretely describe a time in your life when you experienced a true romance.

_____
_____
_____

When, and from whom did you learn the meaning of love and courtship?

_____
_____

What emotional lessons did you learn from your first dating experience?

_____
_____

Explain how you view the activity of voyeurism?

_____
_____

Describe how your addiction has affected your relationships lifestyle?

_____
_____

Discretely explain what you would consider to be the greatest temptation in your life at the moment.

_____
_____

Please explain what you believe to be the difference in love and lust.

_____

_____

TRUE
or
FALSE

Truth    Meter

Answer the following questions to the best of your ability. Some of these questions may be on the quiz at the end of the Pathway.

Please answer the following questions to the best of your ability. Write your answers in the spaces provided.

1. The feeling of being in love is one of those purely _____ experiences.

2. It has been said that _____ is an institution and love is blind, so, marriage is and institution for the blind.

3. The _____ _____ of our society has produced a false sense of what real courtship is and how two people are supposed to act within the parameters of a dating relationship.

4. _____ is the process where two individuals begin the journey of emotional and physical discovery that lasts a lifetime.

5. The process of courtship and dating should be _____ and kept pure.

6. The degradation of _____ _____ has resulted in illicit sexual deviancy on many levels.

7. The mainstream media has also _____ the use of sex as a means of advertising and marketing.

8. This decline in personal _____ _____ has led to an unprecedented increase in sexually transmitted diseases and a drastic decrease in societal standards.

9. As Christians, we know the hope of America and the world is _____ in and through Jesus Christ, and not the increase of moral or social values.

10. The _____ of Jesus Christ is the only things that will bring a society back to moral purity.

11. The results of an addiction to pornography can grow far beyond _____ and divorce; it can lead to a perverse lifestyle that destroys all semblance of normality.

12. As the _____ of the Holy Ghost, we are to remain pure and free from sinful behaviors of fleshly indulgence.

270

**Think about it!**

This area is for writing your thoughts and feelings about the information in this lesson. Please be honest with yourself. This exercise will help you understand and retain what you have read.

Thoughts and Feelings:

_____

_____

_____

_____

_____

_____

_____

_____

_____

_____

**Lesson Verse: Proverbs 18:22**

*"Whoso findeth a wife findeth a good thing, and obtaineth favour of the LORD."*

**Review**

271

This is where the rubber meets the road. You must ask yourself how you will respond to the lesson.

Choose what you believe is the appropriate answer for you, and/or give an explanation of your answer in the space provided. Circle the answer where appropriate.

What kind of person do you believe you are, as revealed by your relationships?

_____
_____
_____

Would you say that your relationships have been sources of strength for you or sources of bad influence? Explain.

Strength
Bad influence

_____
_____

What do you believe the people closest to you would say about your reputation?

_____
_____

Explain the difference in reputation and character.

_____
_____

Explain what you believe to be God's best for you concerning a mate; personality, character, spiritual maturity, etc.

_____
_____
_____
_____
_____

Please answer the following questions to the best of your ability. Write your answers in the spaces provided.

1.  Next to receiving Jesus Christ as your Saviour, choosing your _____ with others is one of the most important decisions you can make.

2.  Your relationships reveal what kind of person you are and what your ultimate _____ in life are.

3.  Your relationships will either be a source of _____ for you to help you do the right things, or they will be the means of tearing you down and influencing you to make wrong choices.

4.  Choosing who your friends are is one of the most revealing _____ into who you really are.

5.  The kind of friends you choose reveal the kind of _____ you have.

6.  The right kind of friends will tell you when you are _____, hold you accountable for doing right and genuinely care about the choices you make in life.

7.  The right kind of friend will want to get to know who you really are so they can help you take _____ steps toward your goals.

8.  Real friends are more concerned about being right than they are about being _____.

9.  The right kind of Christian friend will _____ you when you make mistakes and help you live a close relationship with Jesus Christ.

10. You give God your best by _____ all that you are and may become to Him, allowing Him to lead and guide your life as He sees fit.

**Think about it!**

This area is for writing your thoughts and feelings about the information in this lesson. Please be honest with yourself. This exercise will help you understand and retain what you have read.

Thoughts and Feelings:

_____

_____

_____

_____

_____

_____

_____

_____

_____

_____

**Lesson Verse: Jude 23**

"And others save with fear, pulling them out of the fire; hating even the garment spotted by the flesh."

## Review

This is where the rubber meets the road. You must ask yourself how you will respond to the lesson.

Choose what you believe is the appropriate answer for you, and/or give an explanation of your answer in the space provided. Circle the answer where appropriate.

Describe the circumstances surrounding a time when you lost a position of employment.

_____

_____

_____

Explain how long it took for your addiction to begin controlling your actions and behaviors.

    Immediately

    Days

    Weeks

    Months

_____

_____

How has fellow employees influenced or affected your addiction behaviors? Positively or negatively? Explain

    Positively

    Negatively

_____

_____

What lessons have you learned about how other people influence your actions and behaviors?

_____

_____

What do you feel is the best response to people that would influence you in a negative way?

_____

_____

TRUE
or
FALSE
Truth    Meter

Answer the following questions to the best of your ability. Some of these questions may be on the quiz at the end of the Pathway.

Please answer the following questions to the best of your ability. Write your answers in the spaces provided.

1. Even though the addict knows right from wrong, they still make choices that bring about _____ that many times result in extreme emotional damage to them and their family members.

2. Physical damage includes organs of the body as well as the _____.

3. The most common organ damaged by alcohol is the _____.

4. You must make the choice to not engage in activities that lead to the _____ of relationships.

5. The choices you make right now can and will affect the _____ you will have with your spouse, children and other family members.

6. Your relationship with the _____ is the most important of all relationships.

7. Making the choice to live a _____ life, according the Word of God, is the right choice to make for yourself and your family.

276

**Think about it!**

This area is for writing your thoughts and feelings about the information in this lesson. Please be honest with yourself. This exercise will help you understand and retain what you have read.

Thoughts and Feelings:

_____

_____

_____

_____

_____

_____

_____

_____

_____

_____

_____

Lesson Verse: Matthew 6:11

"Give us this day our daily bread. "

## Review

This is where the rubber meets the road. You must ask yourself how you will respond to the lesson.

Choose what you believe is the appropriate answer for you, and/or give an explanation of your answer in the space provided. Circle the answer where appropriate.

277

What does the fact that God is in control of everything, mean to you?

_____

_____

_____

Explain what it means to you to have faith in God.

_____

_____

As you understand it, what is the greatest thing we can do to prepare for eternity?

_____

_____

What do you believe is meant by, worshipping God?

_____

_____

In your own words, why should we tell other people about Jesus Christ?

_____

_____

TRUE
or
FALSE

Truth    Meter

Answer the following questions to the best of your ability. Some of these questions may be on the quiz at the end of the Pathway.

Please answer the following questions to the best of your ability. Write your answers in the spaces provided.

1. The greatest knowledge anyone can have is the knowledge of ___ .

2. Believing what God says about Himself, with all the characteristics that we read about in His Word takes an act of _____ .

3. We must believe that God is who He says He is, and believe the _____ He has given us about Himself in the Bible.

4. Our life on earth is just a _____ for where and how we will live throughout eternity.

5. If we live only for what we can ____ in this life, we are missing the whole point of why God created us in the first place.

6. God created us to _____ and fellowship with Him.

7. When we acknowledge God as our Father, He responds with love, care and _____ .

8. Because we are born again into the _____ of God, as a member of His family, we should be more concerned with the things that concern God.

9. When we read and study the Word of God, we are opening our minds to the _____ ____ of God for our life.

10. Since God knows all things, He also knows the _____ .

# PATHWAY 14 - Review Test

1. Other than the relationship we have with the Lord Jesus, the most important relationships we can have are with _____ and friends.

   _____

2. Sin always _____.

   _____

3. The _____ of Jesus Christ is the only things that will bring a society back to moral purity.

   _____

4. Next to receiving Jesus Christ as your Saviour, choosing your _____ with others is one of the most important decisions you can make.

   _____

5. The kind of friends you choose reveal the kind of _____ you have.

   _____

6. Real friends are more concerned about being right than they are about being _____.

   _____

7. The most common organ damaged by alcohol is the _____.

   _____

8. Your relationship with the _____ is the most important of all relationships.

   _____

9. The greatest knowledge anyone can have is the knowledge of ___.

   _____

10. God created us to _____ and fellowship with Him.

   _____

# PATHWAY 15
# MOVING FORWARD

## MILSTONE 82
## FORGETTING THE PAST

**Think about it!**

This area is for writing your thoughts and feelings about the information in this lesson. Please be honest with yourself. This exercise will help you understand and retain what you have read.

Thoughts and Feelings:

_____

_____

_____

_____

_____

_____

**Lesson Verse: 1John 2:8**

"Again, a new commandment I write unto you, which thing is true in him and in you: because the darkness is past, and the true light now shineth."

## Review

This is where the rubber meets the road. You must ask yourself how you will respond to the lesson.

Choose what you believe is the appropriate answer for you, and/or give an explanation of your answer in the space provided. Circle the answer where appropriate.

Describe what you consider to be a normal state as an individual.

_____

_____

Explain how far away from "normal" your addiction has taken you?

_____

_____

How does the word "hope" relate to your addiction recovery?

_____

_____

At what level do you believe "false logic" has taken over your thinking processes?
    None
    Some
    Much
    All

_____

_____

Have you come to the realization that addiction behaviors do not have to rule your life?
    Yes
    No

Describe at what point you had this realization?

_____

_____

Answer the following questions to the best of your ability. Some of these questions may be on the quiz at the end of the Pathway.

Please answer the following questions to the best of your ability. Write your answers in the spaces provided.

282

1. What is the definition of recovery? A _____ to normal state; a gaining back of something lost.

2. The word _____ is most often used in context with drug or alcohol addictions.

3. Once the addict is firmly in the grip and bondage of a particular addiction, there is a transfer of _____ that moves from the logical to the illogical.

4. A daily time with the Lord gives us a purpose for life and a plan for the _____, because it is designed by God, for our good and for His glory.

5. Let the past _____ in the past.

**Think about it!**

This area is for writing your thoughts and feelings about the information in this lesson. Please be honest with yourself. This exercise will help you understand and retain what you have read.

Thoughts and Feelings:

_____

_____

_____

_____

_____

_____

_____

_____

_____

_____

**Lesson Verse: Philippians 3:14**

"I press toward the mark for the prize of the high calling of God in Christ Jesus."

## Review

This is where the rubber meets the road. You must ask yourself how you will respond to the lesson.

Choose what you believe is the appropriate answer for you, and/or give an explanation of your answer in the space provided. Circle the answer where appropriate.

For you, what is the most exciting part of taking a trip? Why?
Planning
Leaving
Traveling
Experiences
Returning

_____

_____

_____

Do you have a plan for your future?
Yes
No

If you answered yes to the previous question, briefly explain your plan.

_____

_____

If you answered no to question 2, briefly explain why you feel you have not planned for the future.

_____

_____

At what level do you believe you should allow God to direct you in planning for the future?
None
Some
Most
All

_____

_____

Explain where you feel you are in the Biblical model of the addiction cycle.

_____

_____

What opportunities do you see the Lord opening for you in the near future?

_____

_____

Do you like change? Why?

Yes

No

_____

_____

**TRUE** or **FALSE**

Truth ● Meter

Answer the following questions to the best of your ability. Some of these questions may be on the quiz at the end of the Pathway.

Please answer the following questions to the best of your ability. Write your answers in the spaces provided.

1. If you give God His rightful place in your planning, the resulting _____ will be of His choosing.

2. Because God desires to give us His best, all we have to do is place ourselves in a _____ to receive His best.

3. Regardless of the details of your plan, it is of utmost importance that you recognize the need to seek _____ from God.

4. You must learn how to set realistic goals before moving to more _____ goals.

5. Every addict must make a _____ to start their recovery process.

6. If the addict has learned to follow Christ, _____ will happen in the timeframe God sets, with the right experiences for each individual.

7. We heal by focusing our _____ and efforts on the needs of others.

8. _____ change as we change.

9. The only person's _____ you should be concerned about is yours and the Lord's.

10. Realizing God's help in your life means to honestly recognize even the small blessings, not just the large events where God _____.

**Think about it!**

This area is for writing your thoughts and feelings about the information in this lesson. Please be honest with yourself. This exercise will help you understand and retain what you have read.

Thoughts and Feelings:

_____

_____

_____

_____

_____

_____

_____

_____

_____

_____

**Lesson Verse: 1john 4:16**

"And we have known and believed the love that God hath to us. God is love; and he that dwelleth in love dwelleth in God, and God in him."

## Review

Choose what you believe is the appropriate answer for you, and/or give an explanation of your answer in the space provided. Circle the answer where appropriate.

288

After you complete this course, in what way will you help others receive help from life-controlling habits and behaviors?

_____

_____

_____

Do you view this course as a temporary solution to your addiction problems, or as a permanent one? Why?

Temporary

Permanent

_____

_____

Do you believe the addiction recovery ministries of local churches are more effective than secular programs? Why?

Yes

No

_____

_____

**TRUE** or **FALSE**

Truth Meter

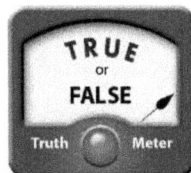

Answer the following questions to the best of your ability. Some of these questions may be on the quiz at the end of the Pathway.

Please answer the following questions to the best of your ability. Write your answers in the spaces provided.

1. Jesus was the greatest _____ that we could ever have to learn what it means to live for others.

2. Once you have received the help you need to overcome your addiction, it is necessary to help others to continue the _____ and growing process.

3. The methods employed in most recovery programs today are useless in terms of a _____ resolution to the addiction problem.

4. Because the Church is the "Pillar and _____ of the truth," it is in a unique position to offer lasting help to the addict.

5. A daily, meaningful relationship with Jesus Christ is the only _____ for lasting freedom from addictions.

290

**Think about it!**

This area is for writing your thoughts and feelings about the information in this lesson. Please be honest with yourself. This exercise will help you understand and retain what you have read.

Thoughts and Feelings:

_____

_____

_____

_____

_____

_____

_____

_____

_____

_____

**Lesson Verse: 2Peter 3:18**

""But grow in grace, and in the knowledge or our Lord and Saviour Jesus Christ. To him be glory both now and for ever. Amen."

## Review

This is where the rubber meets the road. You must ask yourself how you will respond to the lesson.

Choose what you believe is the appropriate answer for you, and/or give an explanation of your answer in the space provided. Circle the answer where appropriate.

How much control over your life are you willing to give to God?
    None
    Some
    All

_____
_____

Explain how much pride you believe you have had in your life in the past?

_____
_____

Describe what it means to you to have humility in your life.

_____
_____

Describe any circumstances in your life where you felt like a victim. When, where, why, how. etc.

_____
_____

Do you feel that you are moving forward in your life, or backward? Why?
    Forward
    Backward

_____
_____

What behaviors in your life do you know that you should simply "put away?"

_____
_____

Answer the following questions to the best of your ability. Some of these questions may be on the quiz at the end of the Pathway.

Please answer the following questions to the best of your ability. Write your answers in the spaces provided.

292

1. God chooses to extend _____ to us because of who He is, not because of who we are.

2. _____ is simply recognizing that God is in control.

3. The feeling of guilt and shame over your addiction can also create an emotional response of _____ or insecurity.

4. Even under _____, we make choices that reflect what we feel will bring about our desired outcome.

5. Growing in grace is accomplished over time through the study and _____ of God's Word to your life.

6. The world views many privileges and _____ as rights.

7. The person that has a heart of humility gladly receives what is given form God, recognizing the _____ of man and the _____ of God.

8. We must recognize that true rights are not given to us from other men or governments, but are only given to us by a _____ and merciful God.

**Think about it!**

This area is for writing your thoughts and feelings about the information in this lesson. Please be honest with yourself. This exercise will help you understand and retain what you have read.

293

Thoughts and Feelings:

_____

_____

_____

_____

_____

_____

_____

_____

_____

_____

_____

**Lesson Verse: 1John 4:4**

"Ye are of God, little children, and have overcome them: because greater is he that is in you, than he that is in the world."

## Review

This is where the rubber meets the road. You must ask yourself how you will respond to the lesson.

Choose what you believe is the appropriate answer for you, and/or give an explanation of your answer in the space provided. Circle the answer where appropriate.

How do you view the importance of making restitution?

_____

_____

_____

To how many people do you feel you need to make restitution?

None

A few

Many

_____

_____

Explain why you believe there may be some people that will not respond to your attempts at restitution.

_____

_____

How important do you believe is God's grace toward you in this restitution process? Why?

None

Some

Greatly

_____

_____

Please answer the following questions to the best of your ability. Write your answers in the spaces provided.

1.  If you are to regain a balance in your life, you must seriously consider the act of making _____ to those who you have hurt along the way.

2.  Restitution is about _____ recovery and is just as important to your mental restoration as much as stopping your addiction behaviors it is about your physical recovery.

3.  There is a great satisfaction in living a life of _____ and strong character.

4.  Your mental state or _____ will determine who and what you attempt to restore first.

5.  Restoring _____ takes time.

6.  _____ is the key to restitution just as it is to the whole restoration process.

7.  _____ always destroys the vessel that contains it.

8.  Restitution and restoration is a journey of humility and _____, but the rewards are well worth the effort.

9.  Whether you realize it or not, _____ is also about the other person moving on with their life too.

296

**Think about it!**

This area is for writing your thoughts and feelings about the information in this lesson. Please be honest with yourself. This exercise will help you understand and retain what you have read.

Thoughts and Feelings:

_____

_____

_____

_____

_____

_____

_____

_____

_____

_____

**Lesson Verse: 1john 1:9**

"If we confess our sins, he is faithful and just to forgive us our sins, and to cleanse us from all unrighteousness."

## Review

This is where the rubber meets the road. You must ask yourself how you will respond to the lesson.

Choose what you believe is the appropriate answer for you, and/or give an explanation of your answer in the space provided. Circle the answer where appropriate.

297

Explain how important forgiveness is in your personal restoration process.

_____
_____
_____

In your own words, explain why it is important to spend time with the Lord every day.

_____
_____

Describe a situation where you have not forgiven another person.

_____
_____

Honestly explain why you have not forgiven this person.

_____
_____

Explain why God should forgive us if we are not willing to forgive other people.

_____
_____

TRUE
or
FALSE

Truth    Meter

Answer the following questions to the best of your ability. Some of these questions may be on the quiz at the end of the Pathway.

Please answer the following questions to the best of your ability. Write your answers in the spaces provided.

1. _____ sin in our life separates us from fellowship with God.

2. Death is both physical and spiritual _____ from God.

3. As a child of God, if we disobey Him, He treats us as ____ __ ____ _____, not as an outsider.

4. You must learn to _____ yourself for your past behaviors.

5. Forgiveness is the outpouring of God's _____ and grace in our life.

6. It is not easy for us to _____ someone who has done us wrong in some way.

# PATHWAY 15 - Review Test

1. A daily time with the Lord gives us a purpose for life and a plan for the _____, because it is designed by God, for our good and for His glory.

_____

2. We heal by focusing our _____ and efforts on the needs of others.

_____

3. Jesus was the greatest _____ that we could ever have to learn what it means to live for others.

_____

4. A daily, meaningful relationship with Jesus Christ is the only _____ for lasting freedom from addictions.

_____

5. _____ is simply recognizing that God is in control.

_____

6. The world views many privileges and _____ as rights.

_____

7. Restitution and restoration is a journey of humility and _____, but the rewards are well worth the effort.

_____

8. _____ sin in our life separates us from fellowship with God.

_____

9. Death is both physical and spiritual _____ from God.

_____

# PATHWAY 16
# CHALLENGES and GOALS

## MILSTONE 88

## FINANCES

**Think about it!**

This area is for writing your thoughts and feelings about the information in this lesson. Please be honest with yourself. This exercise will help you understand and retain what you have read.

Thoughts and Feelings:

_____

_____

_____

_____

_____

_____

**Lesson Verse: Psalm 24:1**

"The earth is the LORD'S, and the fulness thereof; the world, and they that dwell therein."

**Review**

This is where the rubber meets the road. You must ask yourself how you will respond to the lesson.

Choose what you believe is the appropriate answer for you, and/or give an explanation of your answer in the space provided. Circle the answer where appropriate.

In your opinion, what is the purpose of having money?

_____

_____

Try and explain what you believe may be God's purpose for us to have more money than is necessary for our personal needs.

_____

_____

What do you believe how you spend your money tells about yourself?

_____

_____

How many people do you know that you could honestly trust with any amount of your money?

    None

    Few

    Some

    Many

Explain what it means to you to be a steward of God.

_____

_____

**TRUE** or **FALSE**

Truth   Meter

Answer the following questions to the best of your ability. Some of these questions may be on the quiz at the end of the Pathway.

Please answer the following questions to the best of your ability. Write your answers in the spaces provided.

1. Money is only the _____ for addiction behaviors.

2. The cause of the addiction is _____ _____.

3. ___ ___ _____ ____ _____ will determine, in part, how well you recover from your addiction.

4. God instructs us in Malachi that the _____ (10% of our gross income) is holy unto Him.

5. God will bless those who ____ ____ _ _____ _____.

6. Learn to live on a ____ _____ system.

7. What does it mean to honor the Lord with your money? To spend your money to _____ ___ _____ __ ___, rather than to increase personal comfort or pleasures.

**Think about it!**

This area is for writing your thoughts and feelings about the information in this lesson. Please be honest with yourself. This exercise will help you understand and retain what you have read.

303

Thoughts and Feelings:

_____

_____

_____

_____

_____

_____

_____

_____

_____

_____

_____

Lesson Verse: Psalm 122:1

"I was glad when they said unto me, Let us go into the house of the LORD."

## Review

This is where the rubber meets the road. You must ask yourself how you will respond to the lesson.

Choose what you believe is the appropriate answer for you, and/or give an explanation of your answer in the space provided. Circle the answer where appropriate.

What do you believe to be the characteristics of a good local church?

_____

_____

_____

How important do you believe church activities and involvement are to your recovery and restoration process? Why?

None

Some

Very

_____

_____

Explain what you believe to be the purpose of preaching and teaching in the local church.

_____

_____

How important do you believe is preaching and teaching to your restoration process? Why?

None

Some

Very

_____

_____

Explain how important you feel the fellowship of other Christians is to your restoration process.

_____

_____

Explain how an emotional or entertainment emphasis reduces the effectiveness of our church worship services.

_____

_____

305

TRUE
or
FALSE

Truth   Meter

Answer the following questions to the best of your ability. Some of these questions may be on the quiz at the end of the Pathway.

Please answer the following questions to the best of your ability. Write your answers in the spaces provided.

1. We cannot be right with God unless we are right with ___ _____.

2. What is the main purpose of the local church? ___ _____ _____ __ ____
   _____ __ _____ __ _____ ___ ___ _____ _____.

3. The local church is the representation of _____ __ ____ _____ and is led by Christ himself.

4. The meeting of the church body is for the individual Believer to receive
   _____, _____ ___ _____.

5. Teaching is for our spiritual growth, but should never become a substitute for our
   _____ _____ ___ _____ _____.

6. _____ in the church is important because it promotes the unity of the Believers.

7. It is our responsibility to give ___ _____ __ _____ _____ to the world.

306

**Think about it!**

This area is for writing your thoughts and feelings about the information in this lesson. Please be honest with yourself. This exercise will help you understand and retain what you have read.

Thoughts and Feelings:

_____
_____
_____
_____
_____
_____
_____
_____
_____
_____
_____
_____

**Lesson Verse: Galatians 6:2**

"Bear ye one another's burdens, and so fulfil the law of Christ."

# Review

This is where the rubber meets the road. You must ask yourself how you will respond to the lesson.

Choose what you believe is the appropriate answer for you, and/or give an explanation of your answer in the space provided. Circle the answer where appropriate.

What examples of social activities do you feel you could engage in, that would be pleasing to God?

_____

_____

_____

Explain the kind of attributes in a person that you believe other people would respond to positively?

_____

_____

What are some situations in which you feel you would be able to share the Gospel of Jesus Christ?

_____

_____

How important to you is being accepted by your peers? Explain.
    None
    Slightly
    Very

_____

_____

Explain in your own words the importance of having Christian friends.

_____

_____

To what degree would it bother you to no longer be accepted by your worldly friends? Explain.

     None

     Some

     Greatly

_____

_____

**TRUE** or **FALSE**

Truth   Meter

Answer the following questions to the best of your ability. Some of these questions may be on the quiz at the end of the Pathway.

Lesson 90:

1. What is the common misconception about a Christian's social life?

_____

_____

2. What does the bible say in Matthew 5:15-16 concerning this misconception?

_____

_____

_____

_____

3. What does this lesson teach is an important factor in soul-winning?

_____

_____

4. What example did Christ give us concerning our social life?

_____

_____

_____

_____

5. What is the difference between society's idea of a "socially active" individual and God's example of a "socially active" individual?

_____

_____

_____

_____

6. Social behavior is a _____ and _____, which is the foundation of friendship.

7. What is sharing our light, and social life and involvement's one purpose?

_____

_____

8. The world teaches that happiness comes from money, entertainment, and worldly pleasures. What does God promise brings true happiness?

_____

_____

9. What type of friends should a Christian individual have?

_____

_____

10. What is the best decision a Christian can make when it comes to their social life?

_____

_____

# PATHWAY 16 - Review Test

1. Money is only the _____ for addiction behaviors.

_____

2. God instructs us in Malachi that the _____ (10% of our gross income) is holy unto Him.

_____

3. Learn to live on a ____ _____ system.

_____

4. We cannot be right with God unless we are right with ___ _____.

_____

5. Teaching is for our spiritual growth, but should never become a substitute for our _____ _____ ___ _____ _____.

_____

6. What is the common misconception about a Christian's social life?

_____

7. What does it mean to honor the Lord with your money? To spend your money to _____ ___ _____ __ ___, rather than to increase personal comfort or pleasures.

_____

8. The local church is the representation of _____ __ ____ _____ and is led by Christ himself.

_____

9. What does this lesson teach is an important factor in soul-winning?

_____

END

This publication is the Workbook for the Addiction Recovery Program entitled
**"Discovery of Hope" "Biblical Pathways to Addiction Recovery"**

Developed and produced by **Garland Mark Burgess** and
**Transformed Life Ministries**

This Workbook is the companion to the Textbook with the same title:
**ISBN 9780981747453**

This program is also available as a complete 90-day, online program, available at
www.tluonline.com.

For more information about this and other programs or material, visit
www.tlminfo.com.

www.ingramcontent.com/pod-product-compliance
Lightning Source LLC
Chambersburg PA
CBHW081226090426
42738CB00016B/3206